What (TF) Do I Do Now?

What (TF) Do I Do Now?

Reclaiming Myself, One Piece at a Time

Tareasa "Reesa Teesa" Johnson

with Tracey Michae'l Lewis-Giggetts

STOREHOUSE VOICES

New York

STOREHOUSE VOICES
An imprint of the Crown Publishing Group
A division of Penguin Random House LLC
1745 Broadway
New York, NY 10019
storehousevoices.com
penguinrandomhouse.com

Library of Congress Cataloging-in-Publication Data
Names: Johnson, Tareasa author | Lewis-Giggetts, Tracey M. contributor | Title: What (TF) do I do now? : reclaiming myself, one piece at a time / by Tareasa "Reesa Teesa" Johnson ; with Tracey Michae'l Lewis-Giggetts. | Other titles: What the fuck do I do now? Description: New York : Storehouse Voices, 2026. Identifiers: LCCN 2026010179 (print) | LCCN 2026010180 (ebook) | ISBN 9798217088607 hardcover | ISBN 9798217088621 trade paperback | ISBN 9798217088614 ebook | Subjects: LCSH: Johnson, Tareasa | Internet personalities—United States | TikTok (Electronic resource) | LCGFT: Autobiographies Classification: LCC PN1992.9236.J64 A3 2026 (print) | LCC PN1992.9236.J64 (ebook)
LC record available at https://lccn.loc.gov/2026010179
LC ebook record available at https://lccn.loc.gov/2026010180

Hardcover ISBN 979-8-217-08860-7
Ebook ISBN 979-8-217-08861-4

Editor: Jennifer Baker |Production editor: Sohayla Farman | Text designer: Aubrey Khan | Production: Christopher Andrus and Heather Williamson |
Copy editor: Amelia Ayrelan Iuvino | Proofreaders: Julie Ehlers, Navorn Johnson, and Mads Dunn | Publicist: Jennifer Valentin | Marketer: Mason Eng |
Publisher: Tamira Chapman | Associate Publisher: Porscha Burke | Editorial Director: Jennifer Baker | Publishing Associate: Isabela Alcantara | Editorial Assistant: Camryn Johnson

Manufactured in the United States of America

1st Printing

First Edition

The authorized representative in the EU for product safety and compliance is Penguin Random House Ireland, Morrison Chambers, 32 Nassau Street, Dublin D02 YH68, Ireland, https://eu-contact.penguin.ie.

To everyone who thought it was your turn
and it turned out not to be . . . it's still coming.

Contents

A Letter to the Reader

DEAR READER,

For the longest time, I didn't know how to tell my story. I could see the truth but I wasn't ready to say it out loud. I was ashamed, scared, and exhausted from the mental gymnastics I'd been doing for years, trying to reconcile the man I thought I married with the nightmare I woke up to every day.

When I first decided I would share what happened, it wasn't out of bravery, as some people might define it. It certainly wasn't some grand moment of reclaiming my power. Not yet, anyway. Honestly? It was desperation. I felt like I was suffocating under the weight of everything I'd been holding in. So I hit record on that first TikTok video, and I talked. I shared piece after piece of the chaos I'd been through. I called it "Who TF Did I Marry?" because that's the question I'd asked myself, day after day, as my ex-husband's lies unraveled. And it wasn't just that he lied—people lie in relationships. It happens often. It was more about how he lied, how he built an entire universe around those lies and pulled me into it. I became the co-star in his fantasy, and for a while I played my role like a pro. But eventually the mask slipped, and the truth I'd been trying to avoid was staring me dead in the face. The lies. The manipulation. The gaslighting. Every piece of it chipped away at me until I was just a shell of who I used to be. After figuring out who TF I married, it was time for me to finally figure out what TF do I do now, hence the title of this book. I had two options: I could carry the shame and guilt like a uniform I put on daily, or I could face it, acknowledge it, and rebuild.

But first, if you didn't watch all fifty episodes of "Who TF Did I Marry?" here are the CliffsNotes:

I married a man I thought I knew after meeting him via a dating app at the start of the pandemic. Everything moved fast—too fast—but Legion, my pseudonym for him, had this charm about him that made me believe we could build a life together. The first sign something was wrong came just a few months into our relationship, when the purchase of the house he claimed to be buying didn't come to fruition. I also, at this time, began noticing gaps in his stories: where he was from, people in his life, where he once lived, the job he held. As time went on, things got worse. He became more manipulative and controlling, often turning arguments around to make me feel like I was the problem. He actively entered the home-buying process for us with—unbeknownst to me at the time—no money in his account. On top of everything, I later discovered he had been cheating. And when I miscarried our child, I would discover an even more horrifying lie that absolutely crushed me. Despite all of that, walking away from him and our marriage was one of the hardest decisions I've ever made.

I didn't go into my marriage expecting a fairy tale, but I didn't sign up for a horror story either. And when it all came crashing down, I truly felt like I'd lost everything; not just the marriage but my sense of self. I was thirty-five when I married this man, and in that season of my life, I was standing at a crossroads. My biological clock was ticking louder with every passing year, and I felt a sense of urgency to make things happen. To build the life I'd always imagined, by any means necessary. I truly believed I was running out of time. I ignored what seemed like a million and one red flags—so many, in fact, that I coined the phrase "The United Nations of Red Flags." It made me rationalize the irrational, all in the name of love and hope.

But you see, love and hope aren't supposed to rob you of peace. They're not supposed to leave you doubting your worth or questioning your reality. Looking back now, I can admit my faults and the role I played in this delusion. I admit that I settled. I compromised on things I shouldn't have, not because I didn't know better but because I thought I could make it work. I thought I could love him into being the man I needed him to be. Spoiler alert: You can't love someone into healing their brokenness if they're not willing to do the work themselves.

The decision to jump on TikTok and say, "You know what? Y'all ain't even going to believe what the heck I went through with my ex-husband" really did change my life. I didn't think it would. I thought I'd post a few videos, some people would watch them, and others wouldn't. I didn't expect the world to pull up a chair. That said, I don't think I could write this book without including exactly how my life has changed since February 2024. I know now that in telling our stories, we give them room to breathe, and that room makes way for us to be free. Your story may not go viral or be shared a million times like mine, but nine times out of ten, it will impact those in your immediate community and sphere of influence. And all those people will likely have something to say.

When I hit "post," everything erupted. The series went viral faster than I could process it. That's when the comments poured in—thousands of them. Some were encouraging, from women who knew the sting of betrayal all too well. Others were brutal. For the life of me, I couldn't understand how someone could say, "Hey, this terrible thing happened to me," and there could be people out there who would respond with, "No, it didn't. She's lying. She's making that up. She just wants clout." Maybe I was naive, but I just didn't think that was a thing. I thought, *How can anyone tell me that what I experienced, what I went through, never happened?*

Not to mention being called stupid, desperate, gullible, or worse. People said I deserved it for staying as long as I did. They were loud with their "It could never be me" commentary. And let me tell you, those words hurt. They cut deep, because they were echoing the things I'd already told myself in my darkest moments. There is nothing anyone can say to me or about me that I didn't say to myself. They were pricking the old part of me that still wanted to believe I deserved that kind of harm. That I asked for it to happen.

However, in the midst of the noise, the fear, and the grief, I started to notice something else. There were women reaching out to me, not just in the comments but in private messages, saying, "This is my story too. I just didn't know how to tell it." They weren't judging me. They were thanking me. There were even a few sprinkles of men in there, although it was mostly women. And not just Black women either. It was women from every race and sexual orientation. That's when I realized something powerful: Telling my story wasn't just about me. It was about them too. It was about every person who's ever felt trapped, silenced, or ashamed for loving someone who didn't love them back the right way. That's the power of telling your story—you not only free yourself but you just might free someone else. And in that way, none of the negative responses to your sharing really matters, right? The overwhelming good inevitably outweighs the fly-by-night bad. And yet you still must be ready for the bad.

As I said, when my story went viral, life as I knew it changed overnight. On the surface, it looked like a big payback. I was caught up in a whirlwind of opportunity. *Good Morning America*. *Tamron Hall*. A book deal. A TV show deal. But there are other challenges to going viral that many don't talk about. People think it means quitting your job, making a bunch of money, and then sailing off into the sunset. Maybe that's true for some people, but that wasn't my experience at all. I'm asked all the time, "Girl, how are you still working? Why?!" And my answer is pretty simple. Working my job is the most normal thing I have, so I'm holding on to it for as long as I can. I'm grateful for the opportunities, but I'm not going to sit here and act like I don't know that as quickly as they came is as quickly as they can go. Especially in today's political and social climate.

What people don't see is the toll it takes. The sleepless nights. The paranoia. The strangers who think they have the right to dissect your life and your choices like they're episodes of a reality TV show. And the issue of safety is real. There were people who had nothing better to do than to look up my address. I was forced to hire security to go on trips with me. I also had to be mindful of what I was putting out into the world. I can't just drop a family photo on the 'Gram anymore. One woman found my ex-husband even though I never used his actual name. The internet has a way of stripping you bare, and let me tell you, my skin was already paper-thin when it all began. I wasn't ready for the cruelty that came with the spotlight. Beyond the messages questioning my intelligence for staying, I received horrible comments about my weight and appearance. It was like being pelted with stones from people hiding behind screens. Listen, I've always been plus-size. If the people I've encountered throughout my life ever thought I was "fat, ugly, and stupid," they never had the audacity to say it to my face. Up until the response to the series, no one in all my life had ever sent me an email to essentially tell me, "You're fat!" Social media gave people access to me in ways I wasn't prepared for; it gave them a way to say the most vile and disgusting things.

All of it was triggering considering the PTSD I carried from the marriage. Oh, *that* reared its head in ways I couldn't predict. There were moments when I didn't think I would be able to handle it all. Many people might think of post-traumatic stress disorder as something that only happens to soldiers returning from war or people who were severely abused as children. That's not true. Having PTSD from relationships often means we find ourselves unable to trust people. We have difficulty communicating our needs because we are afraid of reliving what we have experienced in the past. I've dealt with all of that and more as I've tried to heal from what happened.

But here's the thing about hitting rock bottom: It forces you to rebuild. Slowly, painfully, but deliberately, I began to thicken my skin. I learned not to give my energy to trolls who only wanted a reaction from me. I reminded myself of the truth: I'm not defined by their opinions or their words. I'm defined by the God who carried me through when I didn't think I could make it. That's what I want you to grab on to as you walk through this book. Maybe this will make you so strong that you will leave that bad situation or share that secret pain. When or if those negative reactions come, I want you to come back here. Remember what I've said. You aren't defined by anyone else's opinion of you. Words hurt, but they don't have to take you out. Stand ten toes down in your humanity, and keep pressing toward your best self.

I've often been asked if I think God put me through this for a reason. Let me be clear: I don't believe God orchestrated my pain. I do believe He allowed it, because free will means we get to make our own choices, even the bad ones. It wasn't His will for me to marry Legion. I made that decision all on my own. In fact, I've often felt like I broke God's heart when I got married. He didn't want that for me, and I lost years to that relationship—years I can't get back. Some days, I do feel robbed. But I also believe that "all things work together for the good of those who love God and are called according to His purpose" (Romans 8:28). And while I made bad choices, I never stopped loving God. I remember sitting in my walk-in turned prayer closet and hearing God clearly saying, "Honey, I did not want this for you. I did not design him for you, but this is what you chose." I also remember my prayer: "God, if what I think is correct, that this man is a pathological liar, then I am in so much trouble. Please get me out of this. I don't know how." I begged God to help me. I didn't know how to fix it, and I didn't even know if I deserved to have it fixed.

But that prayer and confession? It changed everything. It didn't make the pain go away overnight—there was still work I had to do on myself—but it gave me the strength to take the first step out of the darkness. I do believe that now that I'm out of the muck and mess, God is literally taking the ugly rubble of my life and turning it into something beautiful. He can take the ashes of our worst decisions and turn them into something that gives Him glory.

My life right now is nothing but a testimony of God's grace. A little more than a year ago, I was trying to figure out how I was going to renew my lease. I was making payment arrangements with

Georgia Power. Now I'm writing a book. I've become the storyteller I've always been. God saw this hardship coming and knew I'd make my own choices, but what He orchestrated as a result is amazing. He knew I aspired to different things beyond working in a law enforcement office or an Amazon warehouse. He knew I was a storyteller. Maybe He used this season of my life, this experience, to reroute me. To get me back on track as the storyteller I've been called to be.

God knew I would tell this story in a way nobody else could, and that it would blow up my life in the best possible way. At least, I hope that's what's happening. I still don't fully understand the how and why of it all because it's beyond my comprehension. God has a unique sense of humor. And yes, some days I still feel like, *God, I could've been a great storyteller and had a successful husband and healthy marriage at the same time.* Who knows? Maybe that's still on the way. Maybe the healing from this story has to come first, so I'm ready for the husband and everything else that's coming. However it pans out, one thing I know is that I'm not special in this regard. If God did it for me, He will surely do it for you. The question is, will you let him? Will you endure the discomfort, the embarrassment, or any other consequence that might come before you reach the blessing?

This book isn't a retelling of "Who TF Did I Marry?" Sure, I'll spill some of the tea because, let's be real, the stories are wild. (And names have been changed to protect the not-so-innocent.) But more importantly, I'm going to take you behind the curtain for the lessons I learned along the way. Lessons about trusting your gut, setting boundaries, and reclaiming your worth. Lessons about forgiveness and finding your way back to yourself after you've been broken into a million pieces. I'll also break down what I wish I had taken into account as I was going through my experience, in the hope that you will be light-years ahead of me should you find yourself in a similar spot. In short, my plan is to keep it real and be transparent about my shit. Some stories are funny; some are very much not. Some of what I write will be new revelations to the people who know me. But above all, this book will be Tareasa being honest with Tareasa. About how I'm learning to forgive myself, even as God has forgiven me. As Pastor Sarah Jakes Roberts said to me once, it's time for me to stop seeing myself as a cautionary tale. I am a woman who, like so many, made mistakes in her search for love and partnership, but who is deserving of not just God's grace and compassion but my own. I am also a woman who has learned that forgiving herself is the most important form of forgiveness.

Telling my story wasn't easy. It still isn't. Even back in February 2024 when I hit "post," I knew deep down that there was way more to me than those fifty TikTok videos. I'm a real person. Not a caricature. Not a meme. But the ridicule and public scrutiny all made me question whether I'd done the right thing. Every time I doubted myself, though, I considered the people who reached out to me, the ones who said my story gave them the courage to leave, to heal, to speak up. That's why I kept going. That's why I will keep going. If someone sees a little of themselves in me, whether they want to admit it or not, I hope they will learn from my lessons. I don't believe we always have to go through something ourselves. Sometimes we can learn from those who have traveled the road before us.

That's why it's also important for me to say that I'm writing this book from the standpoint of a regular woman who almost bought the lie that I had to be the dumbest person on earth for putting up with all that I did. I *am* a woman who dared to share her story and now her journey. No, I don't have a doctorate from Harvard, nor am I some relationship guru. I am just a human being who had the courage to believe in love and to hope that love had found her. This isn't a self-help book. I'd like to think of it more as a conversation between you and me.

It's funny, because now that I'm on the other side of things and have begun this rebuilding journey, I've been saying that I'm in my "Why not?" era. As I said, my life looks nothing like it did before, and I have deep gratitude for that. But even as I heal from the pain, I'm choosing not to lose that part of me that will always take a leap of faith. The part of me that will say, *What do you have to lose?* My "Why not?" era means I can go on *Good Morning America* and it will be absolutely terrifying, but I still show up for myself. It means I'm going to take that trip to another country; again, it might be scary, but I want to see the world. I want to do the things I've been reading about. If sharing my story allows me to do that, then, yeah, why the hell not? Too many of us don't take advantage of the moment when our life shifts, even when it does so unexpectedly, mostly because of the discomfort and the lack of familiarity with whatever has changed. I'm not doing that anymore.

Here's what I want you to know, right here and now, as we begin this journey together: You are not alone. Whatever you've been through, whatever you're *still* going through, you don't have to face it by yourself. Healing isn't linear. It's messy and complicated. Sometimes it feels like you're taking one step forward and two steps back. But it's worth it. Every tear, every uncomfortable moment of growth is worth it, because on the other side of that pain is freedom.

You're not broken beyond repair. You're not too far gone. Healing is always within reach, no matter how long it takes for you to embrace it. I'm living proof of that. And if you don't believe me yet, I hope that by the end of this book, you will.

Let's unpack the choices we've made and the lies we've believed. Let's examine the wounds we've carried and sift through the ashes to find the beauty that's been waiting for us all along. Because trust me when I say that you deserve it.

LOVE,

REESA

PART 1

What Was Missing

1

I Forgot My Foundation

When you lose sight of yourself,
you lose your power.

LITTLE REESA WAS AMAZING. I know that might seem weird to write, but I think it's worth saying out loud. She was bright-eyed, talkative, and unafraid to dream big. At seven years old, I would imagine myself doing most anything, including Vanna White's job. I'd twirl my little fingers to "turn" the blinds in my grandparents' living room like they were the letters on *Wheel of Fortune*. Or I pictured myself as a sniper stationed in Prague (don't ask me why—I thought it sounded exciting, but apparently my second-grade teacher did not). I always knew—or at least behaved as if—I was going to be some sort of actress. Once I got to middle school and high school, I joined the drama club. My drama teacher even said, "I can totally see you onstage one day at the Academy Awards." Listen, I was extra. I'm *still* extra. And I'm 100 percent okay with that. Reesa Teesa might be new to the world, but my family will tell you that I've always been a storyteller—animated from the very first word to the very last period. The only thing that surprises them is that the world is finally discovering it. They used to love asking, "Tareasa, what happened?" And then they'd listen to me launch into a story, complete with different accents and tones for each character.

I had a gift for seeing magic and possibility everywhere. But what I didn't know then, as a little girl with a limitless imagination who could see possibilities for myself in ways others couldn't, was how fragile that magic could be. I eventually learned that being this way was both a blessing and a curse. You see, I believed I could turn anything and anyone into something beautiful, molding it or them to fit the vision in my head. Whether they truly matched that vision didn't matter. If I could see or speak a thing, I could make the "raw material" of a person or relationship what I needed it to be. And yes, that's a powerful thing when it's harnessed. But without boundaries, it can be a disaster. Over time, those disasters chipped away at my belief in myself, turning my boldest dreams into faint and faded whispers. By the time I met my now ex-husband, I had forgotten how to dream. I had forgotten how to love myself with the same conviction I once brought to imagining my future. I had forgotten the foundation that made me myself.

The thing is, outside of my intimate relationships, I've always had a certain positive sense of self when it came to my body. This is mostly because I usually surrounded myself with people who didn't make me feel bad. Sure, there would be a couple of comments here and there. I remember one time my grandfather said to me, "Oh, if you would just lose twenty pounds, girl, the guys would be fighting over you." But that sentiment was typical for his generation, and it wasn't really something that crushed me.

The truth is, I have always been big. That's simply the world I grew up in. I was raised on fried chicken, pork chops, macaroni and cheese, candied yams, and collard greens. Every woman around me, from friends to family, was plus-size, and I shopped where plus-size women were celebrated. So the issue of chipping away at my self-esteem only came about when I ventured outside of that insular world I'd created—and when my emotions were involved. With the exception of one, most men I was with didn't make me feel bad about my body. But they did try to tear down my self-worth. Maybe those things are connected; I'm not sure. I never saw it that way. All I know is that I was so desperate for a partner, for someone to share my life with, that sometimes I felt the need to accept things I knew weren't good or healthy for me in order to get the love and attention I wanted so badly.

When it came to my emotional self-esteem, most men just wore me down. Nothing ever started out abusive. It was always "Girl, you know I love you. I'd do anything for you" in the beginning. Then, over time, it became "I ain't going to let no other man do anything to you because you're mine." And then that "You're mine" turned possessive in a way that wasn't good at all. It became "You're mine, and nobody else will want you." But by then, of course, I was invested. I was doing whatever it took to make the relationship work. I allowed the words and actions of these men to erode my self-esteem over time, to the point where I was literally a shell of myself. That imaginative little girl inside of me went silent for too long.

When I was a kid, the church we went to held both Sunday morning and Sunday evening services. It was a tried-and-true Black Pentecostal congregation named Power Praise Ministries in Millville, New Jersey. My mom was in the choir, so she had choir rehearsal on Tuesdays. My grandmother was an intercessory prayer warrior, and they had intercessory prayer on Wednesdays. There was also Friday Night Fire, a kind of weekly revival service. If I wasn't at school or at home, I was at church. But the small storefront church of my early childhood was dirt-poor. And so were we. So my mom and I moved to Georgia with my grandparents, and life slowly but surely turned around for us. In many ways, we could breathe better. But what didn't change was the importance and necessity of being in what my grandmother called "God's house."

Back then, though, church was a lot of fun. When we lived in New Jersey, my favorite thing about it was being in the choir. Even though I really couldn't sing, nobody said anything because, frankly, all the kids were in the choir. We'd sit in the pews in our Sunday best, and the congregation would encourage us as we belted out lyrics like, "Father Abraham had many sons! Many sons had Father Abraham. I am one of them, and so are you and you and you. So let's just praise the Lord!" Little Reesa loved it—so much so that she even dared to sing a Christmas solo, off-key and all.

But wait! Let me be a bit more honest here. The choir was probably the *second* thing I loved about church. As I think back, even then, much of my excitement about going was due to some boy I had my eyes on. There was *always* a boy at church I liked, and I *always* hoped my new patent leather shoes from Payless were cute enough for him to notice me.

The church I ended up growing up in down in Georgia was a Church of God denomination, and it was mostly white. That was such a different experience for me, and it took a while to get used to after we moved. Over time, the congregation became more diverse as the neighborhood and city changed. Nevertheless, my family was invested in participating in all of the church's programs. I attended that church all through middle school, high school, and a small part of college before I eventually left and went to a more traditional Black church.

The one thing that never changed about growing up in the church is that I was surrounded by prayer. It was the rhythm of our lives. My grandmother, the fierce intercessory prayer warrior, had a prayer closet where she'd spend hours pouring her heart out to God. When my mom and I lived with my grandparents, I'd often follow her into that prayer closet and take a seat on the floor next to her. I'd start off strong alongside her: "Yes, Jesus! Hallelujah, God! Cover the nations, God!" But eventually, as her voice rose and fell and her words became tangled with tears and conviction, I'd fall asleep right there on her green pillow. She never awakened me as she continued to pray. It was like she wrapped me up in the safety of her faith. Those moments weren't just memories; they were my roots. That closet was where I first learned to believe in things unseen. It was where I felt God most clearly, even though I was too young to fully understand Him.

But as I got older, I let go of that foundation—not all at once but little by little, in ways that felt harmless at the time. I stopped leaning on prayer and started leaning on myself. I started believing that if I wanted something to happen, I had to make it happen on my own. That shift seemed empowering at first, but it wasn't. It was isolating. I had disconnected myself from the thing that kept me grounded. It was a recipe for confusion, for sure, especially when it came to men and relationships. If I'm honest, though, leaning on myself felt like the only thing I could do at that point. Because once I was good and grown, I felt like God was taking too long. In my mind, I kept thinking, *How dare you make me want to be a wife and a mom? Here I am in my thirties, with not even an ounce of eligible options.* I felt like Charlotte on *Sex and the City*, who famously cried out, "I've been dating since I was fifteen. Where is he?!" I used to crack jokes about how my husband's GPS was broken. That he was on the side of the road somewhere and would hopefully be rerouted soon. It didn't help that all my friends had kids and were in long-term relationships. So I said, "Forget it. I'll just find him myself!" It felt right for me to home in on the whole "faith without works is dead" ideology I'd been taught and try to make something happen for myself.

It really didn't matter the man. If he believed in God, didn't put his hands on me, and didn't seem to be cheating, then I was going to say yes if he proposed. I had very few lines in the sand. I didn't talk to God about any of the people I had dated at that point until I was in serious trouble. Then I would pray for God to change their hearts when they acted up. Not once did I ask him to change me. It was as if I couldn't be the problem; it had to be them. And I refused to acknowledge that I hadn't asked God if I should be with them in the first place. That was especially true with Legion. I'd fabricated my healing. I was praying for God to change him, when he shouldn't have been my husband in the first place.

It's not that I had had any major traumatic events in my childhood that made me say, "This is how you're supposed to be with a man. Make yourself small. Don't ask for what you need." I know that is often what people are wondering about when they ask how I ended up in such a terrible situation in my marriage. However, I will admit that part of my relationship with men may very well stem from the fact that I had no relationship with my father. I don't know him; I never met him. The first man whose job it was to protect me, guide me, and love me took one look at me and declared, "She's not mine." Even after a court-ordered DNA test proved I was, in fact, his daughter, he still abandoned me. I'm sure any psychologist worth their salt would say this played a part in how I dealt with men as I transformed from a young woman into a grown woman. There comes a point, though, where I can't blame the absence of a father for the actions of that grown woman. Even more influential in my upbringing was what I saw and heard in the church.

My mom was a single mom, and she dealt with all that came with that. I can't necessarily say that she instilled the idea of marriage in me. She didn't. My mom did, however, instill the idea that I should never have children before getting married, mostly because of her own lived experience. I saw the financial and emotional weights my mother carried as a result of not having a partner. She'd often say, "You see how I'm struggling; I don't want that for you." Marriage and motherhood were always correlated. As far as I was taught, there was no option that looked like "You don't have to be married to have kids." I knew I didn't want to have that life. I didn't want to be a single mother. And I certainly never wanted to be divorced. But I suppose I also had a fantastical view of what it took to be in a relationship that led to marriage. I always thought I was going to meet a guy, we were going to love each other, we would get married, and he would be my best friend. We would go and serve in the church, because that's what you do where I'm from. That's how it was *supposed* to go. The church, via the scriptures, taught me: A man finds a woman, finds his good thing, and then you're off to the races.

Clearly it doesn't always work out that way.

In the environment of my childhood, it was also believed that there was a certain way I had to be in order to get both the ring and the babies. When she was alive, my grandmother used to pick on me because I have tattoos. She'd say, "Please promise me you won't get any more, because a guy is not going to want to marry a woman with a bunch of tattoos." That was the mindset in my household. I suppose this means there was never a time when I thought marriage wasn't the endgame. It was always the ultimate prize—despite not having the best or the most realistic models.

I love my grandmother, and I miss her all the time. She was a force to be reckoned with, and she ran a tight ship in her marriage. But I'm not sure I can say that my grandparents had a happy marriage. On the flip side, there was my aunt, who was the exact opposite of my grandmother in how she moved in her marriage. When she married my uncle after three months of dating, I was eighteen. They didn't tell any of our family that they were going to do it. One day, we just looked up, and they were married. The interesting thing is that she approached her marriage differently than how my grandparents did. From what I saw, she was quiet and didn't argue at all. It was the opposite of what I was used to seeing growing up, and, in a way, I think that was intentional. I think my aunt didn't want a marriage that was toxic and argumentative. But from the outside looking in, as an immature eighteen-year-old, it just appeared to me like my uncle ran things and she didn't have a voice. Obviously now, at this big ole age, I understand that perception is not always reality. What my aunt was actually doing was keeping her marriage and whatever challenges it had private. They had a partnership where they kept their business between the two of them. This was something I picked up when I got married but (clearly) took too far. When I should have been sharing what was going on with my support system, I didn't. These were the examples I had: You were either an extremely demanding or an incredibly demure wife. I'm not sure I ever saw a truly healthy, balanced partnership. So my beliefs about marriage were shaped by that. I knew that my husband and I could not be different religions, because I was taught that we needed to be equally yoked. "Do not bring home an atheist," my family said. "You can bring home a white guy as long as he's Christian," they said. Is he saved, born-again, and filled with the Holy Spirit? That was the criteria. There were other things that played a role in my mindset.

If he had kids already, I was taught that it shouldn't be a big deal. I was supposed to love the kids as much as I loved him. This was the case even though many men were discouraged from marrying women who already had children. Even sadder than that double standard was the things that weren't mentioned. My mom definitely told me I shouldn't let a man hit me. But no one ever said to me, "Hey, when you bring home a guy, make sure he doesn't try to tear you down with his words. Make sure he has integrity and isn't a liar." I get that some may say, "That should have been a given, Tareasa." But I wasn't taught that those were deal-breakers.

The other images that influenced my perception of marriage early on were the ones many of us saw growing up. I watched *The Cosby Show* as a kid and thought *that* was what a perfect marriage looked like. I also watched the pastor and the first lady of my church as they navigated the ups and downs of ministry. From a child's perspective, it always seemed as if their marriage was the ideal. Of course, it wasn't until I became an adult that I understood that sometimes you don't know what is really going on in people's homes. And it wasn't until I became a wife that I understood that sometimes you don't know what is going on in *your* home.

I think that's when I decided to make up my own rules and definitions for marriage. They were certainly influenced by my upbringing and the models I saw along the way, but they were wholly mine in formulation. I didn't think I could mimic Heathcliff and Clair Huxtable because they weren't real people. And I didn't care to replicate the real relationships I had seen. My grandparents, married for almost forty years before my grandmother passed away, were part of a whole different generation, so I couldn't copy that even if I wanted to. Too much about what my grandmother believed "got you a man" (like having no tattoos) was laughable to me. And all the strife and bickering because of how she ran things was not for me. But mimicking my aunt's relationship, which lasted nearly fifteen years before my uncle passed, didn't feel right to me either. I had seen long marriages, but whether or not they were happy, I had no idea. It was also none of my business.

My mom was a different case altogether. She's always said, "If you want to get married, I support you in that, but I don't believe that God made a husband for me." That's her belief. She was never against marriage; she just didn't see it for herself. As a child, I thought that was so weird. Now I realize she was ahead of her time. Today I know more women who are on that road than on the road to matrimony.

I never wanted a marriage where we bickered all the time, and I for sure didn't want a marriage where I didn't have a voice. Of course, I didn't want to be alone either. I guess the reason I ended up in those exact situations in my marriage to Legion was that, while I knew what I didn't want, I wasn't quite sure of what I *did* want. Even more than that, I wasn't sure of what I *deserved*. The one thing I didn't see growing up but that I desperately longed for was a husband I could call my best friend. I'll talk more about that later, but to have someone I could laugh and joke with felt natural to me.

Despite seeing it firsthand, there was never a time when I believed that I could live without being married if I wanted children. It was just the assumed thing. Because of that, in every single relationship and with every single guy I liked, I always had marriage in the back of my mind. *Is this the guy I'll get married to?* I would ask myself. I was the woman who met a guy and immediately imagined my first name with his last name. It was a very unhealthy habit. And no matter how toxic or clearly unhealthy the dynamic was between us, that marriage and baby clock was always ticking.

Now that I think about it, that clock was so loud because I've always associated marriage with a kind of intimacy you can't get in friendships or situationships—a closeness that I've never believed exists outside that kind of commitment. Mature people know that intimacy does not necessarily mean sex. It's something less tangible, but it's powerful nonetheless. It's the feeling of being seen. Of being genuinely liked. There are a few things I can say with confidence, and one is: I know what it's like to be married to someone who doesn't like you. There are no feelings of security there. No sense that there is another person in this world who sees you fully and completely.

I believed that marriage was the place where I could be not only physically safe but also financially and emotionally safe. That's what I think I've been seeking all along.

I won't deny the importance of that financial security to me either. Marriage is important to me because, at this age, I finally understand shit like contracts, beneficiaries, and power of attorney. I understand that "next of kin" means something. I understand that if something happens to him, I don't want anyone else deciding what can be done to him other than me, his spouse. It's a personal choice, but one I never believed I had to make for myself.

But then you look up one day, and you're thirty-three, and for whatever reason, marriage hasn't happened. *Then what?* Honestly, at that point in my life, it felt like God had completely forgotten my name. Like I was on a call to heaven, and all I heard was, "Your call will be answered in the order it was received." I didn't know when or if God would answer my prayers. I guess in some ways, subconsciously, I felt that if I wanted to get married, I was going to have to do it myself, because God was just taking too long. Honestly, that is a very lonely and sad feeling: to see happiness in the lives of the people around you but feel like God has forgotten who you are and what you want. Of course it isn't true, but it felt like it every day of every week of every month.

Even early on in my dating, I carried those idealized views into my relationships. My first serious boyfriend, let's call him Dallas, was ten years older than me. He had three kids by three different women, and I ignored every single red flag. I was twenty-three, and by then I thought I was late to the boyfriend party. All my friends had a boyfriend. I was the only single one, so I believed the lie that I was somehow delayed in that area of my life. Plus I had already begun shrinking myself, twisting into shapes I thought would make me lovable. In the encounters I had as a teenager with boys who were not quite boyfriends, I'd figured out that some of what I was learning from my role models at home and at church wasn't going to get me chosen. So while I was still going to church, I was also picking and choosing the things that I thought would get me the kind of love and acceptance I wanted. In the four years Dallas and I were together, we were always long-distance. He refused to move to Atlanta, but at one point I considered transferring colleges to be closer to him. I could talk more about that relationship, but suffice it to say that I was in love with the idea and the potential of Dallas. That is, until his words of affection turned into words of possession.

Despite only being in my twenties and the relationship having turned toxic, I *still* thought I was going to marry Dallas. Sure, there was no excitement or butterflies at the thought of it, but I'd been broken down by his verbal and emotional abuse so much that I was willing to settle. I had been taught by the church that marriage should always be the end goal, no matter what. I remember telling my best friend at the time, “Maybe this is just the best I can do,” and the look on her face told me just how much I’d broken her heart with those words.

She said, “Reesa. What are you talking about? You are intelligent. You don’t have any kids with this man. There’s nothing to tie you to him. Do you really believe this is the best you can do?”

Yes, yes, I did.

Now, at forty, I just want to hug that twenty-three-year-old version of me. I wish I could tell you I held on to that lesson, that I immediately returned to my foundation after that first relationship, but I didn’t. Mostly because I don’t think I ever considered what it truly meant to live with that kind of behavior for the rest of my life. I couldn’t consider it. I also don’t remember ever seeing myself ending a relationship because I wanted to meet the person God actually intended for me. That wasn’t it at all. In every relationship I’ve had, it’s always just been, *Well, maybe this is him.* And then the relationship would end, and I’d meet someone new and think, *Okay, maybe THIS is him.* And so on, and so on.

It was a singular conversation with a friend that changed everything for me. One day, while we were chatting on the phone, my friend casually mentioned that he was going on a family trip to Hawaii. Something happened to me when I listened to him describe his plans. My longing showed up. It was the first time I realized that I wanted family vacations, shared holidays—the life I had always dreamed of.

As simple as it sounds, that was a turning point. It was the moment I realized what I really wanted. I found myself staring at thirty-five and wanting more from the men in my life. That conversation made me say to myself, *Enough is enough. I'm ready to get married. I want family vacations, family holidays, and trips. I want a family.* That biological clock was ticking louder than ever, so I decided right then that I was done with casual relationships. I wanted marriage. I wanted stability. And I was willing move my line in the sand in order to get it. Basically, I was prepared to compromise.

Many people have asked me for a deeper reason. They think it couldn't have just been my biological clock driving my willingness to compromise for marriage. But honey, it ain't really deeper than that. And let's be honest, I'm not the only woman who has felt the ticking of that clock. We are born into a world where we know about our biological clock starting from health class in elementary school. And if you grew up in the Black church, it's even more ingrained in you. According to the mothers of the church, you need to get your kids out of the way by thirty-five. And if you want to do it God's way, which is marriage first, then children, you were told to be mindful of your age. Yeah, yeah, yeah. I know nowadays we hear all kinds of stories about women having children into their forties and even fifties. Janet Jackson is the one people like to mention to me all the time. But you know what? Janet has help. Let's acknowledge that many people who choose to have children late in life can afford the assistance to do so. They have a team of doctors and nannies and money for private school.

When I looked up at thirty-four and saw nothing but situationships in my life, I knew that what I really wanted was that suburban house with the SUV, driving 2.5 kids around to their various after-school activities. So I moved into overdrive to get what I felt was the ultimate prize. Bending over backward and accepting less than I deserve is what I thought I needed to do to get the very specific thing I wanted. I believed marriage and motherhood would get me a defining kind of love and acceptance, and I was willing to do whatever I had to do to get it, not really realizing that "doing whatever" would make it impossible to get.

Granted, at twenty-five, my mindset was a little different. I thought I had time. But when thirty-four and then thirty-five came, I truly believed I was running out of it. I said to myself, *Look, if you want a family vacation, you need a family. If you want children, you need a husband. If you want a husband, you need to go find him, because God ain't moving fast enough.*

But how exactly do you meet someone nowadays? That was the burning question in my mind. Most of the people whom I'd dated I had met through work or through a friend. Based on my experience, I instinctively knew I wasn't going to meet anybody in either of those places. This led me to creating an online dating profile. I thought, *Okay, I'm going to finish out the rest of 2019, and at the beginning of next year, I'll start online dating and see what happens.*

So I created a dating profile after my birthday in February 2020, and I went all in. I tried Facebook, Hinge, Match, and Coffee Meets Bagel, to name just a few. I was so active on these sites because I was ready. I kept telling myself, *I'm going to meet my person. I'm going to meet someone who wants the same thing as me: marriage and family. I am dating with intention.* Well, I met Legion, and we know how that went.

Listen, I latched on to that man like he was the answer to my prayers. Because honestly, that's what it seemed like. At first, he seemed perfect. He was charming, attentive, and everything I thought I was supposed to want. From the first date, it was clear to me that we wanted the same things. But there were warning signs, even in the beginning—small lies, inconsistencies, things that didn't quite add up. I ignored them, just like I had ignored the red flags with Dallas. I told myself I was being paranoid, that I just needed to trust him. I gave him benefits of the doubt that he hadn't earned.

Remember now, I still had the running dialogue of *you need to be married to have kids* in my head. In my mind, time was running out, and I needed to get this wife and mom thing going. That urgency was driving me and influencing my decisions, or rather my indecision. It wasn't even about whether this was the person God had in mind for me anymore, because I was past that point. Then once he moved in and started looking at houses and talking about marriage, it felt like I was on track. When I found myself pregnant, it was literal torment. I felt like a failure. There I was, on the way to getting everything I thought I wanted, and I'd just fucked up the order. *Now I MUST get married!* I never really pressured him about it—he was very much on board with us getting married, and he even led the charge—but inside, I'd become obsessed with the subject of marriage. The voice in my head said, *You waited all this time only to shack up, get pregnant, and have a baby before getting married?* I had done the very things I swore I'd never do.

It wasn't just in my relationships where I learned to shrink myself to get something I thought I wanted. At the time, I was working at the Georgia State Patrol, which was essentially, in my opinion, a good-old-boys organization. I used to say that I worked with a bunch of old white men whose attitude was, "I knew your granddaddy. Tell that *boy* I said hi." In that kind of environment, I absolutely learned to shrink. I could be funny, but I couldn't be too funny. Smart but not too smart. It felt like I'd always be a nigger to them, but they needed me to behave like a professional one. And yet I stayed there, for a good long while, because it was a stable career with job security, and that was very important to me. No, I was not making a lot of money, but I knew I got paid on the fifteenth and the last day of the month.

I stayed in my lane, for sure, but I also knew their policies like the back of my hand. I figured out that the only way to fight that type of establishment is with its own rules. Even then, it was hard to bring my full self to the office. In 2017, I had an issue with a supervisor who'd written me up. But because I understood the policies, I made an appeal further up the chain of command and was able to retain my employment. I was exhausted afterward, though. After the investigation closed, I consciously made the decision to just be quiet, do my job, and keep my head down. I wore my mask faithfully and daily.

I didn't *have* to shrink myself with my family, but I suppose in a way I did. I didn't have to do that with my friends, but again, in a way I did. I never shared with them how I felt tortured about being alone and unmarried, with no kids. I didn't feel like I could express that to them because I knew what they'd say. "Well, honey, you just need to get on your knees and ask God to send you your husband." "You need to put yourself out there more." Or worse, "Maybe it's not God's will for you." I didn't want to hear all that, so I didn't bring it up. I couldn't share with them the true nature of my heart: I hated my life. I hated coming home to an empty house. I hated working two jobs when I could have been in a relationship where we each worked one. I hated having Saturdays where I had no one to hang out with. And yes, I hated that I didn't have kids. Did I want to hear some real advice? Even some real spiritual guidance? No, I wanted to hear what would align with the bullshit I was telling myself.

The thing I realize about all of this is that somewhere along the way, I'd not only forgotten my foundation—that inquisitive creativity I had as a child—but I'd also forgotten the strength I'd witnessed in my grandmother's prayer closet all those years ago. That faith had once been my anchor. I'd forgotten the most powerful thing I had at my disposal: my ability to pray. Instead I tried to fix everything myself, and the harder I tried, the more lost I became.

More than just my grandmother's prayers, I'd also watched God come through for my mother. She did the best she could as a single mother—and I'm sure there are things she went through that I wasn't aware of. I didn't know how she paid the rent, how she got to work after her car was repossessed, how she gave me school supplies even though she didn't have any money. I distinctly remembered those situations and saw the result, but it wasn't until I was grown that I figured out *how* she was able to do it. In short, she cried out to God. Even when my grandmother kicked her out of the house, she watched God show up for her through friends who opened their homes so we could have a roof over our heads. God answered her prayers every time. And there were way too many times when I forgot that He would do the same for me too.

I'm a firm believer that you need to experience God's hand for yourself to really understand how He moves. The way He moved for my mom was not how He would move for me. But He moved nonetheless. Take that issue with my supervisor, for instance. One of the charges was basically a write-up for violating dress code. I was charged with insubordination because my supervisor said I wore flip-flops into the office when he told me I could not, even though many of my white female co-workers did so often. It was such a surreal experience that day when I had to go before the colonel to explain the charges. I remember sitting in that conference room thinking, *I am a college-educated Black woman who has studied international law and counterterrorism in The Hague, and I am sitting here being reduced to explaining why I wore flip-flops in the office.* They found ways to remind me that, no matter how amazing an employee I was, no matter how many wonderful reviews and commendations were in my file, I was still just a nigger at the end of the day.

What they didn't know was that, throughout that whole process, I was in my prayer closet—not my grandmother's physical space anymore but my own. My mother had just gotten out of the hospital, and I needed that job to pay my bills and help her out. For days, I could not eat nor sleep. I just remember crying out to God, "I'm begging you to handle this for me. I need you to show up and fight this battle for me." And He did. I walked into that appeal with the colonel and spoke from heart. "I am not a liability. I am an asset to this agency," I said at one point. Not only did I keep my job but the colonel created a position for me in another department and moved me. And when my co-workers asked me, "Girl, how did your job get saved?" my only answer was "By the grace of God."

That was 2017. And for some reason, by 2020, there was a disconnect between my prayers for my job and the prayers I should have been making about my desire to be a wife and mother. Especially since prayer had always been my foundation.

I've had enough pastors and prophets tell me, "Tareasa, you have the gift of prayer." My grandmother once wrote in my yearbook, "My God had told me that you were going to bring joy to this family." My mom used to tell anyone who'd listen, "My daughter knows how to pray, but she doesn't use that weapon until things have gotten so bad." Somehow she knew what I would later come to learn. I am still the little girl with the big imagination who spent hours in that prayer closet with her grandmother. I am the woman who has seen God come through for her as soon as she truly surrendered to Him. I knew it was time that I stopped waiting until the twenty-third hour to use this gift of mine.

But there's a reason why I often chose to wait—one I'm sometimes afraid to admit.

You see, I know that if I pray, "God, if this person isn't for me, remove them," God will answer it right away, and that's terrifying sometimes. Because let's be honest, there are people we don't want God to remove from our lives. For whatever reason. I could have used my gift at the beginning of my relationship with Legion. I could have said, "God, if this man is not for me, remove him," and God would have done it, just like he did it with Dallas. But I couldn't bring myself to do it, because the desire for even a shred of what I thought was love was too strong. It's the part I still kick myself over the most: If I had just said that simple prayer, I would have been saved from a whole bunch of mess. The power was there, but my desire for the life I pictured was stronger.

So many of us forget the very weapon we've been given to fight through our hard times, for so many reasons. Sometimes we're afraid for these people to leave us because they're meeting a familiar need. It could be loneliness or the fear that our time is running out. And we know that if God does what God does, that person could leave, and we aren't ready for it. We aren't ready to not get those needs met in that way anymore. Like I learned growing up, we have to be willing to return to our "first loves." In this case: ourselves, our families, our dreams. I suppose, for me, that might mean the creative, imaginative version of myself from childhood—the one who loved to tell stories.

If I'm honest, though, I've had a hard time figuring out what parts of myself I want to return to. In my interview with Robin

Roberts for *Good Morning America,* she asked me, "What do you miss about the old you?"

I said, "I miss being excited." That was true. I miss the innocence of just being excited for the next thing to come into my life, without the awareness of all the pain and heartache. I miss the bliss of being happy—of really believing that every woman, regardless of our size or color, deserves to meet a man who adores us. That when we put good into the world, good will always come back. Unfortunately, *because* of the relational hardships in my life, I can never be that person anymore. I don't have the luxury of that naivete anymore. My marriage made it so that I don't feel safe getting excited anymore. My first love was the belief that when I met someone, it would automatically be my turn, and even though we would go through hard times, both of us would still want it to work. In this new life of mine, that's not a reality. But that's okay! Because even better than returning to a first love is healing enough to create new, better loves. That's the journey I'm on. That's the new foundation I'm building alongside my old one.

When we walk away from our roots, we inevitably feel unmoored and ungrounded. We start to grasp at things that were never meant to hold us. In Matthew 7:24–27, Jesus speaks about the importance of a strong foundation, saying, "Everyone who hears these words of mine and puts them into practice is like a wise man who built his house on the rock." Without that foundation, the storms of life will wash us away.

My life with my ex-husband was a storm, and I weathered it without the rock I had been given as a child. I had forgotten the weapon of prayer and the truth that God's plan for me was greater than anything I could imagine for myself. And because I forgot, I fell. Hard.

But here's the good news: It's never too late to rebuild. To shore up our old foundations or build anew alongside them. It's never too late to anchor yourself in the truth of who you are and whose you are. For me, that meant getting back on my knees, back to the prayer closet, back to the God who had never stopped waiting for me to come home. I'm not going to assume that you believe the same things I do or that prayer is your strong suit. So in that case, what is *your* anchor? What will *you* return to when you are ready to rebuild your life? Because I believe we all have something. Plus, there are a myriad of tools and resources out there to help us get back on track. One of the things I wished I'd done more of, in addition to prayer, is turning to my support system and truly listening to their concerns. Sure, we know that everyone won't be happy or agree with our choices. And no, I don't think you should necessarily do what other people want you to do. But sometimes those closest to you, those who truly love you and want the best for you, can see things you cannot. Things you don't want to see. And laying your pride aside to listen can be the difference between more pain and freedom. I wish I'd felt free enough to talk to my friends more. Or even to make new relationships with people who might have been better equipped to offer healthy, useful guidance. There were way too many times when I felt inclined to say "We're fine" or "I'm okay" instead of sharing my heart and hurt with the people I know would have tried to support me. So even if you're not a praying person, simply building or turning to your support system can help tremendously.

Little Reesa didn't necessarily know how strong she was, but she believed in possibility. She believed that she could have the best in life. Somewhere along the way, I lost that belief. But as I've rebuilt my foundation, I've started to find Little Reesa again.

I've started to dream again, to imagine a life that isn't defined by pain but by purpose, that isn't mapped out by an outdated perception of tradition.

If you feel like you've lost yourself, I want you to know that you can find your way back. I'm a witness. It won't be easy, and it won't happen overnight, but piece by piece, you can rebuild. For me, that looked like returning to and examining my foundation. I recalled the things that had once grounded me and the things that didn't serve me anymore. In doing so, I was reminded of who I am. Now I'm working on doing better at turning to my community. And even building a new one. There are people in my life who I know care for me, so I'm learning how to allow them to hold space for my pain and grief.

Don't know where to start with all this? Let me give you a jumping-off point. Here are a few reminders for the beginning of this journey: You are worthy. You are enough. And God's plan for you is so much greater than anything you could ever create on your own. Let's get back on track.

2

I Chose the Dream When God Was Showing Me the Truth

The Spirit is there to save us from heartache.

IF I HAD LEARNED WHAT I needed to from the relationships I had before meeting Legion, if I had honored the signs and chosen not to ignore the very real interventions God kept placing in front of me, there would have been no TikTok series. No marriage that should never have happened. No viral heartbreak. If I had allowed myself to heal—truly heal—I would never have ventured down the path I've ended up on. Instead I would have been a woman who had finally listened to her spirit and walked away.

But I didn't.

I ignored what was being revealed to me. And not just once—repeatedly. I looked God in the face, heard what He whispered, felt it in the pit of my stomach, and said, "I really want this, though." I thought my desire was more urgent than His wisdom. I believed my life's plan was more important than what God was trying to show me. I bought into the lie that I was running out of time. The notion that if I did everything right, I would be off the market, in a house, and living my dream of having a family.

The truth is, most of the evidence we need to walk away from relationships that don't serve us doesn't come wrapped in thunder or a big, bold NO. Sometimes it's subtle: A closed door. A flat tire. An uneasy feeling. A soft whisper of *Don't go there*. But I bulldozed through every one of those moments, chasing the dream of being married and having a family of my own, no matter the cost.

Each time I chose the story I made up in my own mind instead of the evidence and truth that lay before me, it led me deeper into a cycle of deception and pain. Ignoring the divine revelations, the interventions of the Spirit, doesn't ever protect us. We don't escape the consequences of our disobedience or disregard. In fact, it only prolongs the inevitable or, worse, excludes us from the blessings that might be waiting for us when we do listen.

The first time I ignored God's voice in a romantic relationship was with Dallas. Remember him? My relationship with Dallas wasn't just my first real relationship; it was probably my most toxic. I realize this is saying a lot, considering what I've revealed about my marriage. It was a long-distance relationship, and it was verbally abusive as hell. This man talked to me like I was a dog most of the time, but I let so much go in the name of loving him. My self-worth was in the pits of hell during this relationship. My self-esteem, which had once been in decent shape, was in the ICU hooked up to a ventilator, barely holding on. As I said before, it was less about how I looked—he seemed to love that—and more about how he made me feel. I felt so out of sorts most of the time with him. I was always fighting to be loved the way I needed to be.

In hindsight, I probably should have known that my relationship with him was not going to work out from the start when I realized we didn't share the same religious beliefs. Now listen—I firmly feel that everyone is entitled to believe what they want about God or to believe nothing at all. But I was raised Pentecostal. Sunday morning, Sunday night, Tuesday choir rehearsal, Wednesday intercessory prayer, Friday night fire. I grew up in the church. And according to many of my conversations with Dallas, up until a certain point, so did he. He led me to believe that he was the saved man I was told I should want. So imagine my surprise when we were getting ready to eat dinner and Dallas said, "Allahu Akbar," which means "God is great" in Arabic. I was totally confused.

"Wait, what?"

He shrugged.

To be clear, Dallas was not a Muslim. He used to say that he simply identified more with Islam than with Christianity. And while he never verbally professed his own Christian faith, I had assumed we were on the same page based on how he described his upbringing. But for the first time, at that dinner, I wasn't sure. This was a warning.

It wasn't about what religion he practiced. It was about what that difference represented—how deeply we were misaligned in values, in worldview, and in purpose. Hearing Dallas pray to Allah did not make it clear that I should end our relationship. *Maybe he is just on a spiritual journey. That's okay, right? Many of us question and explore our faith in different ways. What kind of person would I be if I judged him because of that?* Yes, there was that voice in my spirit that said, as clear as day, *That's not your husband.* But of course, I did not listen. I continued my relationship with Dallas, which ultimately led to a level of toxicity that still shocks me to this day—one that probably would have existed no matter what spiritual background he had.

The first time Dallas cursed at me, I froze. I told myself it was a one-time thing. Our relationship had been going on for years, and I wasn't quite ready to end things. But it kept happening. Name-calling. Manipulation. Gaslighting. And still I stayed, because I thought love was supposed to be hard. I thought, *Maybe this is just how grown-up relationships work.* But it wasn't.

The thing is, Dallas started off as a really sweet and respectful guy. He was always very possessive, but he was possessive in a way that seemed lovable, like a "You going to always be my woman" type of thing. It ended up being extremely toxic though. No, he did not put his hands on me. But when you know better, you do better. You accept better. I loved Dallas. I really did. And I thought he loved me as best as he could. What I mean by that is, when a guy cracks jokes like, "Girl, you dumb as hell," and you don't know better, you might not realize those words are a sign of more to come. Whenever he'd say these awful things to and about me, I'd kind of go, "Man, whatever," instead of nipping it in the bud—because I loved him, and because I'd seen his respectful side before. But because I didn't nip those "jokes" in the bud, they started to grow.

I fully believe it was only a matter of time before it escalated to physical abuse because the verbal abuse was so bad. A joke here, a joke there, a "Bitch, what?" type of thing. And the first time you get called a bitch, if you don't address it in a way that demands respect and sets a boundary, it becomes routine. I *never* defined boundaries with Dallas. And because I didn't, the relationship got completely out of control. He took my lack of boundaries as permission. I cannot tell you the number of times that man called me his "bitch" or some other godforsaken derogatory term. Whenever the mood hit him, he turned me into his verbal punching bag, and eventually I became numb to it all. It didn't even faze me.

God was showing me who Dallas was. Repeatedly, the Holy Spirit was revealing to me signs of his poor character and his inability to be the kind of boyfriend I deserved, but as per usual, I chose not to listen. I held on to the good moments, though they were increasingly few and far between, because I didn't want to see the bad moments for what they were. I held on to Dallas's "potential," ignoring the ugly reality that was in front of me.

In fact, at one point he said to me, "I own you. I made you." He was ten years older than me, and he manipulated me in a myriad of ways. And I *still* considered moving to his city to be closer to him. My aunt used to say, "Y'all have this ghetto love, which horrifies me." She was not wrong. I wanted to get married. I wanted to have a kid. Interestingly enough, Dallas was one of those guys who, if he could have, would've trapped me with a kid for the purpose of being able to say, "I'm going to always have you in my life."

For a good portion of our relationship, Dallas would break up with me, and I would beg him to take me back. He'd then say things like, "Bitch, you're going to have to work for this." And I would cry on the phone and promise to do better until we were together again. One time, he didn't come home when I was visiting him, so in a fit of rage, I changed my flight, packed my bags, and took his PlayStation and all his games with me when I left. He called me, almost in tears—not because he had lost me but because he'd lost his damn PlayStation and games. He threatened to call the police on me if I didn't return everything to him. But I had already sold everything as soon as I got off the plane. And sadly, we were not done with each other.

Another time, a woman somehow found my phone number and

called to tell me she'd been messing around with him for about a year. When I confronted him about it, he broke up with *me*. Yes, you read that right. He was more upset that I had stayed on the phone with her, that I had had a conversation with the woman, than about anything else.

"The fact that you even entertained that tells me everything I need to know about you," he said.

And still we weren't done. Not yet. Because I was naive, and I was refusing to listen to all the evidence God was carefully and regularly laying out before me. To be honest, I was so far gone in that relationship. I don't know whether to hug that version of myself or absolutely knock her upside the head.

It wasn't until my grandmother passed away that something switched in me. The day my grandmother died, grief cracked me wide open, and it gave me new sight. Dallas wasn't there for me, physically or emotionally. He didn't come to the funeral because he had appendicitis and he had to have his appendix removed two days before. Maybe that would have been a reasonable excuse in a healthy relationship, but for me, it was the final straw. My grief was so heavy, and I needed someone to help me hold it. If I didn't know anything else, I knew that's what a partner was supposed to do. But Dallas wasn't there for me, and that was finally my out. Maybe I was looking for one all along? Who knows. All I knew was, in that moment, my heart was broken. This woman who loved me, who had helped raise me, who was the Thelma to my Louise, had passed away. My last memory was of her seeing me graduate from college in May 2011. She sat in that assembly hall and beamed with pride as I walked across the stage to get my degree. By the end of June, she was gone, and my life felt like a very sad, dark place. There are days when I'm glad she wasn't here to see the fuckup of my marriage, but there are other days when I'm deeply sad that she didn't get to see her ReasaMae become Reesa Teesa. She would have gotten a kick out of this ride I'm on. But back then, I didn't want to hear all about Dallas's woes and how I wasn't there to take care of him after his surgery. I didn't give a fuck about any of that, because half my heart was gone.

I said to myself, *Why are you putting up with this? She would not want this for you.* That's when I finally heard the Spirit, whom I had ignored for such a long time, loud and clear: "Leave."

I knew that in order to make a clean break, I had to go completely cold turkey. No calls. No contact. Nothing. I knew Dallas would not expect that. He didn't believe I'd ever have the strength to walk away from him. And he wasn't entirely wrong. I literally asked God to take the desire for him out of my heart, and God did. We broke up in the middle of my lunch break at work one day, and my last words to him as he was cussing me out about something or another went like this:

"Dallas?"

"What?" he spat.

"Go fuck yourself."

Click.

Within fifteen minutes of hanging up, I'd called Sprint, changed my number, and removed him as an authorized user (I know, I know). I blocked him on all my social media accounts. I erased all aspects of him from my life—all by the time I clocked back in from my lunch break. It was insane just how quickly the light switch went off. But I'm grateful it did. I'm also sad that I didn't take the time to heal. Oh, I played Trina's "Single Again" until I wore the song out, but I wasn't healed. And because I didn't heal, I didn't learn.

About three years after Dallas came Beavis. (That's an inside joke; a nickname he and I had for him.) With him, the devil chose a different tactic.

Deep sigh.

There would be no Legion without Beavis. Let me just start right there, because it's the ugly truth. Beavis was THE guy. The nice guy. The "safe" guy. He was a corny, funny gentleman who was also a lovable country boy at heart. He lived for his University of Georgia football and his Chick-fil-A sweet tea. And it was like he came out of nowhere. I had been feeling that ever-present desire for companionship, so when Beavis arrived, I was ready. He, on the other hand, was going through a nasty breakup at the time. Nevertheless, I convinced myself that I had been sent to help him heal. *Hello there! Captain Save a Hoe, reporting for duty.*

I started working for Georgia State Patrol as a dispatcher in September 2013, and I met Beavis in March of the following year. After a brief initial encounter, we exchanged numbers and started chatting. We would yap away while he was working, texting each other back and forth for as long as four hours. Texting ultimately turned into talking on the phone. He would call me throughout his six A.M. to two P.M. shift up until about five P.M., when he'd go to sleep until one A.M. He would text me "Sleep?" and I, of course, would pretend to be wide awake so we could talk more. It was by far the most natural friendship I had had with a guy.

Finally, one day Beavis said, somewhat randomly, "I'm going to come over to your house." I didn't take him seriously, nor did I think he meant anytime soon. But sure enough, this man showed up at my apartment the same night wearing a white SEC (Southeastern Conference) T-shirt, some red basketball shorts, and black Crocs. I cracked up laughing when I opened the door and saw him standing there. That evening, we did nothing but watch TV like an old couple. Like people who had known each other for years. We sat there laughing, trading stories, and talking shit to each other. It was one of the most memorable times I had with him. In that moment, we were genuinely just friends who talked to each other every single day, and as I've mentioned before, that was always one of the things I longed for most in my relationship. In my mind, this was how it was supposed to be. Everything clicked. It was easy.

Beavis was also very supportive. He was the kind of guy you brought home to meet your family. He asked about my day and showed up when I needed him. I once had an unexpected visit from "Cousin Flo" at work and had no pads. Guess what that man did? He went to Kroger, bought me some pads, and brought them to my office. He was that guy. He would call just to hear my voice and shoot the breeze. Did I mention that he didn't have kids? Zero. None. To be honest, that played a big part in me falling for him.

He also asked for my opinion on things and respected my thoughts. If something happened to him, I was the first person he would call. He confided in me, and I did in him. For six months, that's all it was between us: friendship. Beavis was "my person," no question about it. He made me feel safe, and he made me feel seen. In fact, if someone had asked me at the time, I probably would have described him as my best friend, and *that* was new for me. He never disrespected me, and he never called me out of my name. It was just a breath of fresh air. You mean there was someone out there, a man, who actually cared about my well-being? Who seemed to want the best for me? Sign me up.

But I completely misread all the signs. I took his engagement in our friendship as a sign that he might have been feeling something more for me. Probably because he'd tapped in to all the things I wanted in a relationship, and if you combine that with my deep desire—hope, really—to be married, what you get is a woman who is inevitably getting ahead of herself. I named the relationship before he did and conflated our platonic intimacy with romance. That's never good.

But Beavis isn't off the hook either. The fact that we talked every day, spent quality time with each other, and talked about what the future would look like made me think we were on the same page. Why would you do all that with someone who is just a friend? Although we were never in an official relationship, I'd built an entire fantasy around what we *could* be, and he never stopped me, despite the fact that I know he sensed it.

Even with the feelings I had started to develop, I still made the worst decision: I became physically intimate with him. Once sex was introduced, all logic left the conversation. If I was truly honest with myself back then, I would have stopped the relationship from progressing further after that first time we slept together. The truth is that we weren't physically compatible—at all. Nevertheless, I told myself, *Sex isn't the most important thing.* It was more important to me that we could laugh, have great conversations, and build a future together than whether or not he blew my back out. As crazy as that may sound, it's even crazier for me to admit. As a grown woman, I know who I am, what I enjoy sexually, and what I want, and yet I chose to demote myself in that area.

I did have some reason to believe that even if we weren't "together, together" in that moment, we were heading that way. Beavis and I talked all the time about having kids—McKayla would be our first daughter's name, then Mya and Alyssa would follow. For crying out loud, the man gave me a Christmas card signed with his name and the names of our three "daughters." We said we would buy a Cape Cod–style house, where he would have a man cave decked out in UGA football gear. Surely that meant we were a couple, right? I thought so.

Well, no, it turns out. Because the fact was that he never said that. No matter what else was said or done, he never officially made me his woman.

Okay, sure, he had never dated a Black woman, let alone a plus-size Black woman, before. But what did that matter, right?

Well, apparently it mattered *very* much.

I really think God was throwing everything at me at this point. Anything to get me to see that this man, as much as I cared for him, as "safe" and as "good" as I believed him to be, would not and could not reciprocate my feelings in the way I deserved. It felt like God used Beavis's vulnerability to show me the qualities that should have been my non-negotiables. Like the fact that Beavis held all these stereotypes about what it meant to be with a Black woman, despite him coming from two Black parents who were very much still married. In our conversations, I could tell he'd bought into the podcast bros ideology that Black women were "too much" or "always in your face." But of course, instead of listening to what God was showing me and releasing my feelings for Beavis—hell, even running as far away from him as possible—I did what many women do: I tried to prove him wrong. Reality, however, was slapping me left and right.

I was a friend with benefits who behaved like I thought a wife should behave. I was loving and kind and helpful. I never raised my voice. I walked him through his hard times. I spoke life into him, and did everything I could to be perfect—to try to show him that I was different from the stereotype he had in his mind.

"I'm so proud of you," I'd say.

"I know you can do it. I believe in you," I'd say.

I was so far gone over my "friend" that I would leave encouraging notes in his car for him to find, with words that would build him up. It was all a recipe for heartbreak.

The way I often describe my pseudo-relationship with Beavis is this: He was essentially like a broken-down car stuck on the side of the road. Despite every indication that I should just move on and get something new, or at least something that needed less work, I was the mechanic who took him to my garage and put in a new engine and transmission. I made it my mission to restore that car to pristine condition, all shiny and smelling good—even though the cost of doing so was way more than the car was worth. I just knew I was going to look so good driving this ride that someone else had thrown aside. And I did it all because I wanted him to pick me. Yes, even as I was trying to change the views he held about Black women, I was absolutely guilty of being a classic "pickmeisha."

In my defense, I was in love with Beavis in a way that I think was very pure. I really didn't want anything from him—at least not anything that would hurt. I just wanted to marry this man and pop out about three kids. I wanted those family vacations, romantic trips, and anniversaries. I wanted college football Saturdays and trips to Ikea in his pickup truck. I wanted to see our kids run to the front door when their daddy's car pulled into the driveway. And there went that imagination of mine. I saw my whole fantasy life with this man, and I loved him wholeheartedly and with every fiber of my being. I truly believed we were going to be together—eventually. No one could convince me otherwise. For me, he was the guy. Even if he didn't make me speak another language in bed.

I think there might have been a part of me that, until recently, subconsciously believed that since Beavis didn't call me a bitch or make me cry daily in order to make himself feel better, the relationship with him was worth pursuing. Beavis never called me out of my name. He never raised his voice at me. He was the complete opposite of Dallas, and I was enamored by that. Imagine wanting the butterflies-in-the-stomach, fairy-tale romance but not *really* believing it was meant for you. As a result, you might do a lot of compromising. A lot of defining your healing by the acceptance of very basic things (Oh, he doesn't yell at me!) as opposed to what I deserved as a woman (Oh, he loves me with abandon, and I feel it in every part of me).

On Fourth of July weekend in 2016, nearly three years after we had met, reality came and slapped me upside the head. Beavis came to my house—yes, he had a key—and told me that he'd met someone in a Walmart parking lot and now he was ready to see what was "out there."

I was devastated. It was the kind of heartbreak you feel in your bones. After enduring that blow, I couldn't eat or sleep. It was such an all-consuming pain—the kind that changes how you breathe. I cried until I couldn't cry anymore. Sure, the 2025 version of Reesa would have seen this coming. She would have said to that younger version of herself, "Yes, he was acting like your man, but he never *said* he was your man. He never claimed you. Baby, the signs were there. You just ignored them because you wanted him to pick you."

Back then, every bit of discernment I thought I had was apparently turned off. Every new wrench God threw into the mix throughout my time with that man was deftly blocked like I was some desperate-to-be-married Black girl ninja with great skin and fabulous lacefronts. I was utterly blinded by my desire to be accepted and loved by this "good man." So naturally, when he said to me, "I want to see what's out there," I wanted to scream back, "I'm right here, motherfucker!! What do you mean?" It broke me. I can't and won't sugarcoat this. I was so far gone that I often found myself listening to the late, great Angie Stone's "Wish I Didn't Miss You" on repeat and belting it out until my voice was hoarse. I stayed at work late to avoid going to the home he had helped me pick out. It was the worst heartbreak I'd ever gone through. Clearly, my ex-husband was like, "Hold my beer," but at the time, I'd never felt rejection quite like that.

I was also confused, because hadn't I done everything right? I was supportive, loving, and attentive. I was doing everything I thought a man would want in a partner. Everything *except* listening when God was showing me that this was, in fact, not the man He wanted for me.

To a certain extent, though, I think some of my confusion was valid. It was hard to think that this guy would talk about baby names, the type of house we would live in, and what our marriage would be like if he wasn't serious. What I didn't understand was that talking about these things was easy for him. It didn't require him to extend himself beyond our pillow talk or our private conversations. He didn't have to hold my hand in public or change his relationship status on social media. He didn't have to say my name out loud or proclaim his feelings to me directly. He didn't have to claim me. He gave me just enough to keep me hoping for more. And I was 100 percent guilty of underestimating him. Beavis knew how I felt about him, but to him, I was a fail-safe. I was a plan B. He knew that my desire to fulfill the fantasy I'd created in my head meant I would override and ignore whatever divine interventions would ordinarily push me to either let go of him or ask him for more. The Tareasa he knew would always be there. So whenever he wanted to see what was "out there," he figured he could always come back if it didn't work.

If you are an honest person reading this, I implore you to be careful about what you say and do if you are in a casual situation with a woman. If you sense a woman is really feeling you, the last thing you want to do is engage in this kind of dream-casting with her. Do not spend time creating a vision of the future with her. It might even be best for you to be completely honest and reiterate where you stand. Yes, it may hurt her initially, but it will save her a world of pain in the long run.

So guess what I did? I set him free. That's what we have been told to do, right? Sure enough, he would go and date someone for a little while. Then they'd eventually fizzle out for various reasons, and he'd come running back to me for . . . ahem . . . a tune-up. I know, I know. There's a saying that goes, "If you set someone free and they come back, it's meant to be." Let me just say it right now: That's some bullshit. Because Beavis came back every time another woman hurt him, and I kept making the mistake of thinking, *Oh, now he knows that this is where he should be.* But every single time, he'd leave again. Off and on, that is how the cycle continued.

I understand that Beavis is not the villain in my story. He certainly wasn't forthright even though he knew about my feelings for him, but more than pointing the finger at him, I want to own my part in this. I hadn't healed when I met Beavis, though you couldn't tell me that back then. Beavis was a lesson God was trying to teach me. *Pay attention to the signs. Listen to what I'm revealing in this person's words and actions. Don't make up your own story. Don't fill in the blanks with your ideals.*

At every turn, God was showing me what I needed to be careful of and blocking me from accessing a part of Beavis that I really wanted. Even when, way deep down, I knew something didn't feel right, I still chose my fantasy over what was clearly in front of me. I should've walked away the first time I realized I was giving more than I was getting. I should've listened to the quiet voice that kept saying, *This isn't it.* I loved that man more than he loved me. Wait—even more, I loved that man more than I loved myself.

If I had loved myself more, I would have chosen myself. I never would have given him the pedestal that I put him on. I saw his potential but ignored his reality. So I held on—for too long. And when the relationship finally ended, I was broken in ways I couldn't even understand yet. Sadly, this would be a recurring lesson in my life.

When I met Legion in 2020, Beavis was dating someone else and therefore not in my life at all. We only reconnected after I kicked my ex-husband out of the house in June 2021. He'd always said that he would be there for me as a friend if I needed him. He is still the guy you can call at three o'clock in the morning if you're in trouble. But he is also the guy who will block your number if he's in a relationship with another girl. Thankfully, this was a "down" time for him. He came over immediately when I called and asked him to change my locks to keep Legion out. (More on that later.) Let's just say that, unfortunately, not long after he helped me, I was back in the same cycle with him.

The cycle continued as it had before I met Legion, but this time, I was different following my divorce in that I was in a place where I wanted—no, needed—answers. So one night, with Adele's "My Little Love" playing on my Bluetooth speaker, I finally asked Beavis the one thing I had never had the balls to ask before. "Why didn't you ever want a relationship with me before? Was it my attitude? Was it my personality?" He tensed up but remained quiet as I finally whispered, "Was it my size?" He took a long time to respond, but one thing I knew about him was that if you give him time, he will answer. So I waited, and then he said, "Yeah, I guess that was it."

I'm grateful that Beavis was completely honest with me, even if it took him an hour to get it all out. "There's nothing wrong with you, Tareasa. Nothing," he said, in sum. "You are a good woman. Probably the best woman I know. It's just when I think about the type of woman I would be with . . ." His pause told me everything he was about to say, but I wanted to see if he was really going to release the words. "Well, she's smaller."

Yep, that was it. Beavis was never going to choose me, never going to publicly claim me, and it was because I was plus-size. For the record, I knew this. I think I just had to *hear it* out loud. Of course I was good enough for him to sleep with. Good enough for him to emotionally drain me like a vampire. But I was a big girl, and that automatically excluded me from being anything more. Wow. How does a woman really reckon with that? Better yet, how does a woman know this and *still* struggle to let the man go? From the moment he confessed that to me, I quietly resolved that I would never be intimate with him again. And I wasn't just talking about sex. I knew I would never be emotionally open with him again.

As a plus-size woman, this was my first time learning one critical lesson that we all seem to learn eventually: Some men will absolutely enjoy sex with a big woman despite having no intention of being in a relationship with her. They love the benefits. For some, it's even a fetish. But they will never claim her. This was my lesson. Beavis and I went out all the time, but never with any public displays of affection. Not one time did he ever love me "out loud." In fact, he never said "I love you" outside of cracking a joke. He never introduced me to his parents because, as he would say, "I want it to be serious when I do." There was always a small voice inside that whispered, *It's your size.* There was always evidence of it, but I dismissed it. I still felt like all I had to do was be patient and he would eventually see me as "the one." Hold on to the dream at all costs, right?

Something in my gut (no pun intended) told me that his issue was with my size. That's the whole reason I mentioned it to him. But prior to that moment, I could never bring myself to ask him directly. Especially not while we were still doing whatever we were doing. The women he ultimately chose didn't look like me at all. And I wasn't willing to lose half my size just to be with him. So yes, his news was gut-wrenching, but it also caused me to breathe a sigh of relief. *Now I know.*

My relationship with Beavis was another reason why, by the time I met Legion, I was determined to be with someone who outwardly showed they adored me and my body. I didn't want to be anyone's science experiment. Beavis had never been with a plus-size woman, but he clearly enjoyed it.

Legion, on the other hand, was ready and willing to love me out loud. He adored me and praised my curves. He gave me PDAs whenever we went out. In the beginning, he literally handed me everything I had ever wanted from Beavis but didn't get. Legion made me feel chosen, so I never questioned where I stood with him. He made his intentions known and, as they say, that man didn't play about me.

But once again, I mistook all of that for love.

The truth is, I probably would have never even entertained a relationship with Legion had my heart not been broken and still mending from Beavis. Honey, I didn't know real heartbreak until I found myself begging God to heal my heart from Beavis. But God can't heal you when you are still holding on to the very thing that broke you. I never asked God to remove Beavis from my life, which meant I was still not ready for him to be completely gone.

When Beavis found out about me getting married through mutual friends, his reaction was "What? You did what?!" It was almost like he couldn't believe that someone wanted me out loud and in the open. In a way, that was satisfying. I felt like I'd proved him wrong.

So yes, I met and stayed with Legion because the clock was ticking. Yes, I didn't want to be alone. I wanted the marriage and motherhood and all that comes with that. But the more subtle reason that I'm just now coming to realize is that I actually believed myself to be healed enough for a new relationship.

But I wasn't. I was still bleeding from Beavis. From Dallas, even.

And Legion? He looked like the antidote.

Divorce has a way of making you truly examine yourself. I wish I could say that I finally listened to what God was showing me with Dallas and Beavis, that I decided for myself to leave these situationships on my own terms. Unfortunately, it took enormous grief with Dallas and devastating rejection from Beavis for me to get even close to the point of letting them go. And I know that if I'd somehow gotten what I wanted from either one of them, I would not have been happy—especially with Beavis. Maybe I would have been content. Things might have been okay. But in my heart, I know there would have been a stagnation that would have torn me apart from the inside out. If God, instead of constantly trying to get me to see that I deserved more, just said, "Okay, you can have him," it would still not have been His best for me. Because, listen, I prayed for that very thing to happen. I was on my knees saying, "Please change his heart. Please let him want me." And if God had said, "Fine, Tareasa. Here!" I would have spent the rest of my life in a relationship with someone who ultimately would not have made me happy physically. I would have been like Miss Celie in *The Color Purple,* staring blankly at the ceiling as Mister "did his business." Listen, I hate that I lied to that man by telling him he's the best I ever had. I made him think he was rocking my world and, in a way, probably unwittingly gave him the confidence to go and see what else was out there. But I was in love, and I did not want to hurt him. That version of love, that version of me, was willing to sacrifice the intimacy I deserved for the stability I longed for. And in the end, I *still* didn't get what I wanted.

By the time Legion came into the picture, I thought it was divine timing. I thought, well, no, this isn't the package I expected, but this man is doing everything I asked God for. Everything this other man wouldn't. It's got to be God!

I'm sure God was like, "Umm, now why am I in it? This ain't me, baby girl."

I know now that I wasn't being honest with myself. The truth was, I was just tired of waiting. Tired of being overlooked. Tired of loving people who didn't love me back. Legion walked in while I was vulnerable, and instead of checking for red flags, I rolled out the red carpet.

And God tried to stop me.

This time, not with observational evidence. Not with things a man would or would not say or do. The Spirit gave literal signs that screamed, "THIS IS NOT THE WAY."

My tire blew out the day of our first date. A sign? Probably. But I pushed through. The first time I caught him in a lie, I rationalized it. "Nobody's perfect." The first time I questioned his finances, he spun a story so convincing that I convinced myself it had to be true. Even when I started getting even more clear signs that Legion wasn't the answer to my prayers that I thought he was, it was easy to ignore them because he *was* the answer to other things I'd prayed for in those previous relationships. So sure, he lied about that thing. And then later about that other thing. Then about that, that, and that. My eyes were still turned toward what I wanted and not what was best—certainly not what was God's best.

Legion's shenanigans didn't happen all at once either. It's very easy to dismiss one red flag because no one's perfect. The problem comes when you have to keep saying that over and over again in order to try to make a person's behavior make sense. I almost feel like God had to allow something bigger and more devastating to happen in order to get me to see what was really going on.

Looking back now, I know that while God didn't cause my miscarriage, he surely was opening a door—a way out. A divine invitation to leave before things got worse. We weren't married yet when it happened. Legion wasn't on my lease. I could've walked away clean. And I *should've* walked away then.

But guess what? I didn't.

I'll share more later about this time in our relationship but suffice it to say that I clung tighter. I told myself that this man had stood by me through grief, and that had to mean something. That's what the man in my fantasy, my dream life, did. As a result, I ended up choosing potential over reality.

To be clear, I still believe in going after love. Give it a try, Sis. Not everyone is going to have the outcomes I had. But also be mindful. Listen, listen, listen to what the Spirit might be revealing to you. Pay attention to what's actually being said (or not said). Deal in truth and truth alone, even if it goes against what you desire in the moment. Trust that God, the universe, your life—whatever guides you—knows best. And yes, sometimes we truly do not have it in ourselves to walk away without some disastrous, heartbreaking event happening. I know I didn't. I've often thought about what any of these men could have done to make me feel empowered to leave on my own. And I'm not sure that the version of Tareasa they met would have walked away under any circumstances, except maybe physical abuse. So divine intervention is often very much needed. That prayer of "God, if he ain't for me, just remove him" is needed. That "Universe, show me what I'm missing" is needed. But again, you must be willing to be led by whatever happens after that.

Here's what I want you to understand, though: The Spirit is always speaking. But sometimes we aren't ready to hear it. We confuse comfort for confirmation and chemistry for calling. We think love is supposed to hurt, so we make excuses when it does.

But God is merciful.

Even when I was knee-deep in lies and manipulation, God never left me. He continued to send little nudges. Gut feelings. Closed doors. Every piece of evidence I ignored was another opportunity to choose myself. And even though I didn't always listen, He kept showing up.

Because that's what the Spirit does.

And when we finally learn to listen—to trust that still, small voice—we find our way back to wholeness. I had to learn to stop praying for what I wanted and start praying for what was *right*. I'm still a work in progress in this regard. I've had enough experiences, good and bad, to know what I want. But my prayer is now that my desires line up with God's will and His idea of what's best for me. I'm learning to stop asking God to change people and start asking Him to change me. To open my eyes and strengthen my discernment. To help me walk away even when everything in me wants to stay.

Slowly, I'm starting to heal. Yes, in real time as I'm writing this.

I'm learning my patterns. The chasing. The over-giving. The loneliness that can sometimes drive me to accept less than my best. I'm starting to ask better questions of myself. How does this person make me feel? Do I feel safe? Do I feel seen? Am I giving more than I'm receiving?

For the most part, I try to live my life according to Proverbs 3:5–6, "Trust in the Lord with all your heart and lean not on your own understanding; in all your ways submit to Him, and He will make your paths straight." That's a survival strategy. Whenever I have leaned on my own understanding, I fell. When I started trusting God to reveal what I needed to know, my steps got lighter.

So here's what I want you to ask yourself:

1. Am I ignoring the signs?
2. Am I confusing desire for destiny?
3. Am I staying in something that's stealing my peace?

If the answer is yes to any of the above, it's okay. You're not too far gone. The Spirit is still speaking. The door is still open. And healing is still available. I'm trying everything in my power not to allow heartbreak to make me hard, and I encourage you to do the same. Let it make us wise. When something doesn't feel right, let's trust that feeling—and then act on it.

3

I Allowed the Fear of Being Alone to Lead

Loneliness should never be the reason you stay.

I REMEMBER THE EXACT MOMENT in my marriage to Legion when I realized that both my desire for the perfect married life and my loneliness had me bargaining with my dignity. Sitting across from Legion in our home, exhausted and grasping for whatever I could hold on to, I said, "Maybe we should have an open marriage."

In March of 2021, more than a year into our relationship and three months into our marriage, I had scrolled through my husband's Facebook Messenger app on his phone. Don't ask me what made me look. I generally do not believe in looking through phones or apps to see if someone is cheating. But for some reason, I did this time. What I found wasn't just flirtation. It was full-blown sexting. Plans. Promises. Pornographic poetry. When I confronted him about the indiscretions, he claimed one woman was his cousin. "That's just how we joke," he said. His cousin! I'd never met this cousin. And any pictures I might have seen of other women were met with "Oh no, remember that's my cousin." Eventually the story changed a little bit more. Now she wasn't his blood cousin but more like his play cousin. After reading those text messages, I can assure you I've never talked with any of my cousins that way, play or not. The other woman? According to him, it was an ex from many, many years ago. Allegedly. An old flame apparently relit in the heat of a pandemic.

It was obvious in the messages—which were a month or two old by the time I saw them—that he had not done anything physically with these women yet. There was a plan to get together once the COVID restrictions were lifted.

"I don't want to do anything because it's too dangerous right now," she wrote. "When they lift the restrictions, you can get this pussy though," she added.

That was the line that made me lose it.

I've known men who very much loved the idea of having the whore on the side because he didn't want his wife or girlfriend to do the freaky things the whore did. It's like the wife is the pristine Madonna and the side chick will indulge all their nastier sexual inclinations. And of course, I can't say for sure if that's what Legion was thinking. But I couldn't help but internalize what I was reading as him wanting something else. Something different. Which was strange to me, because I was mostly down for whatever with my husband. I'd told him many times, "Bro, you got a whole wife who went to FAMU. If you'd let me know what you wanted, we could have done that." But it was very apparent that he was disgusted by even having these conversations with me, even if he had no issue having these conversations with other women.

If I can be honest, I wasn't necessarily torn up about him having these inappropriate conversations and potentially cheating. I wasn't crying out, "How could you do this to me?!" The truth is, by then I was already emotionally detached from Legion. I was tired of questioning the things he said. Tired of questioning myself. Legion and I got married on January 5, 2021, and I knew by January 31 that I was in trouble. By the time March rolled around, there was so much doubt and inconsistency. I didn't know what was real anymore. So I guess I blew up because *I'd* been faithful. I was angry because if that's what we were doing, I could have been getting that same attention—good attention—elsewhere. I had turned down real, viable opportunities in the name of this marriage. I basically said to him, "I'm over here being Ms. Faithful No Matter What, turning down opportunities, and you are over here acting like your dick is Skittles. So just ANYBODY can taste the fucking rainbow? What?!" I had held the line for a man who couldn't keep it in his pants—or out of his DMs.

That day, out of frustration, I said to him, "Look, there are obviously some things you're into that you're not willing to do with me, so I think we should consider having an open marriage. You do you, and I'll do me." I laid it out like a business proposal. "We can keep things intact—publicly. I will never disrespect you. I don't want you to disrespect me. We can just agree that whatever is done outside is never brought into our home." Legion's face twisted in horror at my suggestion. The man who had been sexting women while lying in bed next to me had suddenly found morals.

It was clear to me that Legion was not happy with my suggestion. He kept telling me that open marriage wasn't what marriage was about. The audacity! Of course, I immediately brought up the sexting, but he held to his stance that I was misunderstanding the messages.

I laughed. Not because it was funny but because the hypocrisy was laughable. From what I could tell, what I was proposing was exactly what he wanted. He was doing it anyway, so why couldn't we just be adults about it?

"I don't think I misunderstood anything," I said calmly. "Go have your fun. As long as you get home at the same time every day, I will still cook. I'll still keep this house clean. We will still do things as a couple. We'll still look for a house. But again, you'll do you and I'll do me when it comes to our sexual needs. We don't need to talk about it. We don't need to put it in each other's face."

For me, it wasn't about revenge. It wasn't about being "progressive" or trying to spice up a stale situation. It was survival and desperation. It was me trying to make sense of the nonsensical and salvage a home I had tied my future to. I was already disconnected from him, but I wasn't ready to be alone. Divorce felt like failure. And loneliness? That felt like a death sentence. (More on that in a minute.)

Legion's response to me confronting him about the messages wasn't remorse; it was panic. He seemed more upset about being caught. His idea of damage control was suggesting we go to marriage counseling. Not a therapist, though—a pastor. Someone he deemed as "qualified." That was fine with me, I guess. I reached out to someone I knew: Pastor Drew Franklin, a former co-worker turned chaplain. I remembered him being the kind of man people respected. He'd been married for more than thirty years. He was someone solid. It seemed like everyone at the job had talked to him at one time or another.

Thankfully, Pastor Drew was also a Facebook friend of mine, so I reached out to him and explained the situation. "Do you and your wife do marital counseling?" I asked. At the time, Legion and I didn't have a church home, so there was no one connected to us in that way. Pastor Drew said, "Let me talk to my wife," and eventually they agreed to do the sessions. With COVID still running things, Legion and I began meeting weekly on Zoom with him and his wife, Margaret.

Our first couple sessions were civil—friendly even. Legion participated just as much as I did. From my perspective, he was acting like he actually cared. And the conversations were . . . interesting. By week three, though, the shift came. Whenever I'd look at him, his body language told us that he did not want to be there. His answers sounded clipped to me, like he was over counseling already. When asked, sometimes he claimed he was just tired from work. Whatever was going on, something was off for sure. The man couldn't be bothered to fake it anymore.

Then things heated up. He told Pastor Drew about me saying I wanted to open our marriage. He even had the nerve to sound betrayed.

Margaret's eyes went wide. "Say what now?" She then turned to me. "Now, Tareasa."

I sat there just as calm as could be. "Yes, ma'am."

"Why would you suggest that? Were you serious or just kidding?"

"Well, the truth is, I was serious," I said. "Based on what I read in those messages . . ."

He tried to stop me from talking about those messages, but I kept going.

"No, let me finish! Based on what I read, this is what he's into. But he's not into it *with* me. So I decided we should make our own rules."

"Tareasa, that's not how marriage was designed," Pastor Drew said.

I know. But he already broke the design, I thought.

I stood on my perspective. "I just think this will allow him to get his needs met, and I'll get mine met too."

There was a brief pause before Pastor Drew asked, "Is there someone who is already trying to fulfill those needs for you?"

I stared at him, shocked. *Why in the hell would he ask that?*

"No," I said. "I have not done anything."

Oh, the irony, right? When I suggested the open marriage, I hadn't stepped out. Not once. Plenty of men were trying to spin the block with me, but I had no side piece waiting in the wings. I was just tired. Tired of begging a man to see me. Tired of giving my body to someone who didn't value my soul. Tired of pretending I was okay. I turned the conversation back to where it belonged: Legion's actions.

"Obviously, the suggestion of an open marriage struck a nerve with him. Yet he still doesn't see anything wrong with the messages and videos he exchanged with these women."

Legion conceded that the exchanges were wrong, but then he went back to his favorite way of escaping accountability. He told us that he didn't want to be continually prosecuted for something he'd already apologized for.

"Prosecuted." As if I were the law and he were some poor, misunderstood defendant. I started to correct him and say, "Don't you mean 'persecuted'?" But I didn't. Because it really didn't matter. He believed that because he hadn't physically cheated yet, it wasn't that big of a deal. And I guess I was in counseling because I was also worried that might be true.

Margaret was very frank with me after that session. "I don't have a good feeling about y'all," she said.

And believe it or not, I was confused by her statement. In my mind, I thought pastors were obligated to say, "No, the devil is a liar. We are going to pray y'all through." But she kept it very real. "How long have y'all been married, Tareasa?" I told her that we weren't even six months in. "I don't see y'all making it to six months," she said.

I remember Pastor Drew looking at his wife strangely, as if to say, "Why did you say that?" But Margaret was clear. "This is not God." Her words aligned with something Pastor Drew had said in a previous session: "If you all had come to us before you got married, we would have told you all to end this relationship."

They didn't really go into any more detail as to why, but post-divorce, I now believe they discerned early on that Legion had been lying. They didn't know how far or how deep the lies went, but they knew something wasn't right. It was almost as if they were saying, "We'll continue to help y'all as much as we can, but we don't think God is going to fix this."

WHEN I THINK ABOUT the impact loneliness had on my decision-making in my relationship with Legion, I cannot leave out the role the pandemic played. If there had been no COVID, our story would not have happened. The only reason we chose to live together was because of quarantine. We wanted to be able to see each other frequently and would not have been able to do so otherwise. Obviously, I did not meet him with the expectation that we would quarantine together, but it's interesting that instead of me saying, "Let's get to know each other over FaceTime," I jumped to "Come to my house. Let's live together," after only knowing him for a little more than a month. It would take a long while for me to reconcile the reason: I did not want to be alone. The looming pandemic ensured I would be if I didn't act quickly, and I couldn't fathom that.

Fear of being alone had always been with me, but it usually felt like only a distant possibility or like something that was possible over the long term. But just like it did for many people, the pandemic amplified those fears tenfold. It truncated time and made me feel like I had to choose whatever connection was in front me. Having only met Legion a month before lockdown, I chose him.

Prior to this relationship, I never dreamed of living with a man before marriage. Shacking up was never part of my plan. But I'd heard stories of how easy it was for single people to sink into a deep depression when they had no interaction with people beyond the internet, and I didn't want that. Of course, in the end, there were people who did very well for themselves during the lockdown. They took time to learn a new skill, gain a hobby, rest, or exercise. But there were also people who struggled emotionally and mentally. They felt the isolation intensely. And I'm fairly sure I would have fallen into the latter category. On Christmas Day in 2021, almost two years into the pandemic, I finally caught COVID and had to quarantine in my home for the final week of the year. It was one of the hardest things I'd ever had to do. I was absolutely devastated not to be able to be with my family. They drove to the house and dropped off my gifts and dinner, but only being able to see them through the glass door crushed me. That told me I would not have handled quarantine well by myself prior to that. As I said, I already struggled with loneliness before I met Legion. I could not have held it together day in and day out had I been forced to be almost completely by myself for nearly two years.

It didn't help that Legion was extra cautious during COVID. He didn't want me going out with any friends, even after things had started to open back up. He'd say things like, "I lost my grandmother and uncle, I don't want to lose you too." I would later figure out that it was less about me catching COVID and more about him wanting to isolate me from any friends or family. People who would have probably warned me about him, had I been willing to share.

For these reasons, I firmly believe that things would have been very different if the pandemic had not occurred and we were free to see each other whenever and however. Things would likely have fizzled out quickly between us. I probably wouldn't have gotten pregnant. His lies would have probably been even more obvious when held in the light of other conversations and evidence. Everything Legion told me was a fabrication, but I wasn't able to prove any of it because of COVID. Administrative offices at the college he said he had attended were closed or overwhelmed. Communication with any potential source of confirmation was stilted across the board. As serious as COVID was, it was also a security blanket for us that eventually became an isolation tent. Our dysfunction was like a bacteria that grew exponentially because the environment was right for it to do so.

Not long after that final therapy session, I began finding out just how deep Legion's lies went. When it finally got to the point where I knew I couldn't stay, I sat in the parking lot of Kaiser Permanente in Jonesboro, Georgia, and called Margaret.

"If what I think is true is true," I said, "Margaret, I'm in trouble."

She got really quiet at first. Then she asked, "Why do you feel that way?"

"I just have a feeling I'm about to open Pandora's box if I keep looking for something. Because I'm already finding more than I bargained for . . ."

The whole time I was married to Legion, I kept asking myself, *What am I missing?* It wasn't just about his stories not making sense. It was more like his stories made just enough sense to keep me in a constant loop of uncertainty.

God, what am I missing here?

I'm sure that part of my feelings of isolation while in the marriage were fueled by the fact that I wasn't attending church. But weirdly, the situation drove me back to God in a way that probably wouldn't have happened had Legion and I had a church home. The trials in our relationship drove me right back to my prayer closet, and though it took a good while, that dialogue with God—the questioning, the tears, the documenting of what was happening in my audio journal—was how I survived it all. Even asking for an open marriage wasn't really about me trying to be rebellious. It was me searching for and seeking an answer. I was trying to survive a situation that was unraveling fast, and I was too afraid to let it fall apart.

Many people have asked me why all this confusion wasn't enough for me to leave sooner. The truth is, I really did not want a divorce. Whenever things would come up, I'd get angry for a moment and then allow the issue to fade away enough for me to survive. I saw everything as something that could be worked through, because I knew the alternative was me being alone again. I didn't know how to be by myself and also have peace. Those two things felt like polar opposites to me at the time.

The confusion was my self-doubt rearing its ugly head. His lies made just enough sense to keep me questioning myself. I would say, *Am I just jaded? Am I that messed up that every time this man talks, I think he's lying?* And with most things, there was usually no way to verify whether his story was true or not. So I chose to err on the side of *Surely he wouldn't lie about that.* That made the young Reesa inside of me—who always wanted connection, who thought she needed to be *with* someone to feel whole—content. Plus, without hard evidence, it was just easier for me to keep ignoring and lying to myself.

Let me own this one thing about getting married to Legion after dating him for a while. I did not marry him because I was totally in love. I got married because I'd signed my name to a car I could not afford without his help. I was financially dependent on him. I thought, *I'm thirty-five. I don't make as much as he does. I want a family. If he proposes, I'm saying yes. We'll figure out what we need to figure out later. We'll make it work.* I was an expert rationalizer. *Men lie. Women lie. It happens. But his lies aren't THAT bad.* What I wasn't admitting to myself was that it is a hell of a lot easier to not feel alone in life and living when someone else is helping you carry the bills.

By the time I saw those messages only a few months into our marriage, the excuses were really easy to spin. *Yes, this is a bit of a mess, but we can fix this mess together. Because if we don't, on the other side for me is loneliness, and I'll be damned if I'm going to do all this emotional work, make all the mental concessions I have to make to be with this man, only to still end up alone.*

Again, I've only recently come to terms with just how much that fear of loneliness was at play for me. The fact that I didn't leave at the first, second, or third sign of utter confusion was because I was not willing to be lonely. I was not interested in the sleeping-alone loneliness. The eat-on-the-couch-alone loneliness. That kind of loneliness that makes your body ache for someone's touch. The kind where your phone doesn't ring. Where nobody asks what you want for dinner. The kind of loneliness that makes you feel invisible.

Nope, I couldn't do it. I could carry the lies and confusion way better than I could the loneliness. The latter was heavier in my mind. The possibility existed, however small, of things changing or getting better when it came to the lies. But in my mind, there was no possibility of happiness if I had no one. Of course, the teachings of my childhood reared up too. Didn't the Apostle Paul say, "It's better to marry than to burn"? (Long-term celibacy was not my ministry, so . . .) And I wanted children. Wasn't it always better for kids to grow up in a two-parent household if possible? I refused to let single motherhood be my portion. In fact, I wasn't willing to go back to being single at all. In my mind at the time, it was the worst thing I could ever be. Getting divorced after two months of marriage was absolutely not an option—not over some text messages.

Somewhere in my head and heart, I'd internalized the idea that being married and slightly unhappy was better than being single and, as I saw it, fully miserable. At the time, I put singleness in the same bag as loneliness, and I wasn't willing to carry it. That was my mindset. I truly believed that anything Legion threw at me could not be worse than not having someone at all. I was wrong.

Even now, being single, I have a lot of anxiety around living by myself and being by myself. You hear those stories of women who are found dead in their home and weeks have passed because there was no one to check on them. I have a fear of something like that happening to me. There are moments now when I'm sitting in my house pondering how many days it would take for someone to realize, "We ain't heard from Tareasa." I think that now, and I'm actually on my healing journey. I'm actively working through these feelings and regularly reminding myself that I'm safe and that the likelihood of this happening to me is very slim. I know *now* that, yes, there are worse things than being single. Being with the wrong person, for one. But you can only imagine how magnified those feelings were a few years ago when healing wasn't the goal; companionship, no matter how harmful, was.

That former version of myself was desperate not to come home to an empty house. She thought that if life was going to throw her all these curveballs, she should at least catch them with somebody.

I had also bought the lie of "having it all." I didn't understand why, as a Black woman, I couldn't have what so many white women seemed to get. The husband. The house. The car. The life. The vacations. I wanted the fantasy, so I sacrificed the truth. I sacrificed myself. And despite the evidence in front of me, I really did believe that if I simply contorted myself enough, I could have all these things *with* Legion.

What I couldn't see then was that the loneliness had already arrived. I was lonely *in* the marriage. Lonely in the counseling. Lonely in the house we shared. Lonelier, even, than when I'd been single—because this time, the silence was accompanied by betrayal. By confusion and the quiet grief of knowing the man I had married was entirely different from the one in my head.

What's wild is that I wasn't new to this type of silence. I had been lonely before being with Legion. I knew the ache of coming home to an empty apartment. I knew what it felt like to wonder who would notice if I didn't show up. But I let the fear of being *that* woman—the one who couldn't keep a man, who couldn't make it work—override what God was whispering to my spirit.

And now? Well, when the pessimistic side of me comes out, I get angry and say that all the fantasy I was longing for was me being terribly unrealistic. Sometimes I think I'm just not on the list anymore for the happily-ever-after life package. The train has left the station. But I know that this might just be the pain still talking. The truth is, I have no idea what God might do in these years to come. Sure, the hard pill to swallow is that what I wanted at twenty-five might not be in the cards. I must make peace with that. But that doesn't mean that something greater and more fulfilling is not on the horizon. I have to believe that. I want you to believe that.

Acceptance is incredibly important on this journey to having stronger, better relationships. Making peace with our lives looking different than we imagined is a necessary step toward living lives that are filled with possibility. But I want to honor the fact that, for many of us who desire to be in healthy relationships, getting to that kind of contentment and peace is hard. I know I'm not the only woman who said, "God, you are taking too long. If you give us the desires of our heart, and the desire of my heart is to be married and have a family, where is it? These are things I've wanted since I was a little girl."

So when Legion came into my life, he fixed my tire and said, "Let me make sure you're good," I truly thought, *Okay, he doesn't look the way I thought he was going to look, but I think this is the guy that I have been saying to God I want as a husband.*

But no matter what he looked like, God didn't send him.

All the internet dating gurus say, "If a man wants to, he will. If he likes you, he will pursue you. You do not have to wonder how he feels about you; he will make it known." Of course, that's true. What they fail to caution you about is that liars can do those things too. Liars can pray and quote scripture. I mean, even Satan knows the Bible front to back. Sometimes liars will do exactly what those writers of relationship think pieces tell you they should do, all in an effort to hook you. Then once you're hooked, they turn into someone else, and you have to figure out how to unravel from the foolishness.

My fear of loneliness kept me from sharing the details of what was going on with my family and friends. Even my mother suspected something weird was happening, and she told me that she didn't think I was happy but because I never went into any great detail about what he was doing, she chose to continue to pray for me and trust that God would take care of everything. I didn't share much about what was going on with my family and friends in the beginning because I wasn't willing to hear them tell me I should break up with Legion. I felt like I was too close to getting everything I wanted, even if it came with a lot of turmoil. I wasn't ready to leave. I wasn't ready to be alone again. I wasn't ready for any of the truth telling or background checks that I knew my people would dish out.

After the divorce, I not only struggled with the loneliness I was so afraid of before but I beat myself up over having a failed marriage. *You couldn't even make it a year, Tareasa.*

As I've said, I had long equated singleness with failure. I saw being single as a punishment—something to be ashamed of. I had no idea that solitude could be sacred. Even as I write this, I'm learning that being alone can actually mean being free. That peace, the kind that comes from being whole, isn't found in a partnership. It's found in purpose.

It took time to learn that, though. It was a lesson that first began when I sat in the darkness of my bedroom closet, asking God, "Why did you send me this man?" and hearing nothing but the sound of my own breath. I've had to accept that the marriage I fought so hard for wasn't just broken; it was a lie from the start. But in that wreckage, something else grew. I'm starting to see myself again. I'm starting to hear the power in my voice—a power I'd silenced for so long. And I'm learning that loneliness and aloneness are not the same thing. In fact, I define loneliness differently now. It's the ache that comes from self-abandonment. That pit in your stomach when you know you've stayed too long in the wrong place. The mask you wear to convince others you're okay when you're dying inside.

But aloneness? Aloneness is choosing yourself. It's eating dinner by candlelight even if no one's joining you. Filling your home with music and laughter. Knowing your worth doesn't decrease because someone else failed to see it.

Don't let loneliness lie to you. Because that's what it does. It tells you that you're running out of time. That having *someone*, anyone, is better than facing the silence. It tries to convince you that crumbs are a meal. They're not. You can't make peace with mediocrity by calling it companionship.

I wish I had remembered sooner that God never means for His daughters to settle out of fear. His presence is enough. The Spirit's hand is steady, even when ours shake. Loneliness should never be the reason you stay, Sis. Not in a job. Not in a friendship. And certainly not in a marriage. Don't sacrifice your soul for company.

I come home to peace now. I laugh loudly and freely. I cook what I like, wear what I want, and sleep diagonally in my bed. I'm not trading that for anything less than I deserve.

And yes, some nights are quiet. But I am no longer in a relationship with someone who makes me feel invisible, where my needs are minimized and my intuition is constantly being gaslit. I know now that I deserve more than the bare minimum dressed up as *at least I'm not alone*. I'm still working on not letting my desire for partnership become a prison. It's still challenging to believe I am already more whole than I feel. But what I know for sure is that sometimes the most radical act of self-love is staying single *on purpose*. Not out of bitterness or fear but out of a deep, abiding love for yourself that refuses to shrink into spaces that can't hold you.

4

I Ignored My Gut

Your intuition is a divine gift. Trust it.

MY GUT AND I HAVE A LOVE-HATE RELATIONSHIP. She speaks to me, and, depending on my stubbornness, I may or may not listen. She's been my ride or die since day one—always warning, always nudging. But I've treated her like the friend I only call when I'm already in crisis. And the truth is, I didn't just start ignoring her when I met Legion. I had a whole résumé of gut neglect long before that man ever came around.

I didn't listen to my gut when Dallas was calling me an idiot and I would just laugh it off. I thought, *Who am I to make a big deal out of some words?* I was twenty-three and late to the dating game, so when this man showed interest in me, it felt like the validation I'd been waiting for. Nevertheless, my gut warned me that getting involved with a man who had three kids by three different women was not the move.

But he chose me!

My gut nudged harder when the jokes turned into full-on verbal abuse. "Bitch," he'd say, casually, like it was my name. And still I stayed. Still I tried to prove I was good enough. My gut was practically screaming, but I muted her, telling myself, *This is just how love is when you're grown.* Until it became unbearable. When his words turned from "I love you" to "I made you, bitch, I own you," my gut continued to plead with me to listen to her. She yelled that it was time to go, but I didn't listen, and what happened? I prolonged the heartbreak.

Men who prey on women often choose us when we have limited options in several areas of our lives. It can be when we don't have a lot of freedom, financial or otherwise. Or when we don't have the kind of support system that will intervene on our behalf or help us. Or it can be when we hold so much shame that we aren't going to share with our support system what's going on. These are the targets they love. In the beginning of my relationship with Dallas, I was living at home and under the watchful eye of my mother. While I was there, Dallas's attitude was rather benign. It's only when I moved out and got my own place that the ugly side of him came out, because he felt like he was losing control. There wasn't a way for him to monitor me when I was living on my own and doing my own thing. When I was in my mother's house, he knew I wasn't going to get too wild. There wasn't going to be too much going out, drinking, other men, and whatnot. That control is what he needed to not let his beast show. When it was gone, the beast was free to roam.

Sometimes we so desperately want something to work that we create excuses to justify the things our gut is telling us. I'm a witness to the fact that denying reality only deepens your wounds. Whenever we dismiss that feeling in our bodies—that something just isn't right—we're pretending that the flag is changing from red to green. We're turning it from red to a deeper, richer, bloodier red. I believe that God speaks to us in a myriad of ways, and sometimes He speaks right through the pit of our stomachs. My gut told me something wasn't right—again and again, it sounded alarms I chose to ignore.

And I ignored it when I met Valdosta, a man I met after breaking up with Dallas and before meeting Beavis.

Wait. Now who is this, Reesa?

Exactly.

Valdosta was the complete opposite of Dallas. He was literally the sweetest guy ever. Very much the "yes ma'am, no ma'am," "let me get the door for you" type. And he was *so* protective of me. But for all that sweetness, we had a dating cycle of up and down, on and off. We'd get together, break up, stop talking, then get back together again. It was like we were always being pulled back into each other's orbit, but neither of us ever stood still long enough to say, "We're too grown for this. Either we're going to do this right, or we're not." And when we argued, if there was even a raised voice from him, I'd say, "I'm done." I didn't have it in me to fight. Not after Dallas. I was still carrying the trauma from that, and any hint of tension felt like danger. So I bailed—every time.

It was during one of those "we're not talking" phases that I met Beavis. And, well . . . y'all already know how *that* went.

I share this relationship with you because I've come to an uncomfortable and inconvenient truth. From Dallas to Beavis to Legion, I've been drawn to men who were not quite available to me, whether physically or emotionally. And Valdosta? He was the one who *was* available. And I rejected him, for reasons I'm still unpacking.

There *is* another truth I know now: I didn't choose Valdosta because I wasn't ready for him. Even more than that, my gut was telling me I should try harder with him, but I'd already begun a pattern of doing the opposite of what my gut was telling me, and I wasn't stopping anytime soon. Plus, I got with Valdosta only about nine months after ending things with Dallas. I *thought* I was healed, but I wasn't. That's why every conflict with him felt like a red flag even when it wasn't. Honestly, I also saw him as an option. I loved him, but I was childish enough to believe that I could just spin the block if other things didn't work out. Sound familiar? In my mind, I think I was saying, *Okay, I'll come back to you. If this don't work out, I know I can always hook up with you again.*

Valdosta never forgave me for choosing Beavis. For thinking *he* was the better option. I tried to explain. I told him, "I thought he was. I really did." But he couldn't get past it.

"It's the fact that I'm not a bad dude and you *still* picked him," he said.

That stung. Because Valdosta wasn't wrong. He was so hurt by it all, and I was too. I tried to explain that I wasn't *trying* to hurt him but that I honestly believed Beavis was the guy. Not because he was better but because he was a different kind of nice. Valdosta had alpha energy: assertive but not disrespectful. Just solid. Grounded. Beavis was softer, more accommodating at the time.

I fell in love with the idea of Beavis. He didn't have kids. Valdosta did. Beavis's divorce was pending, sure, but I was willing to give *him* grace that I never gave Valdosta. Even when my gut was screaming, "Um, sweetie, you're the rebound." Of course, when karma spun the block on me and things with Beavis did blow up in my face, I braced myself for the "I told you so" from Valdosta.

"I love you," he said. "But anybody could've seen that once somebody else came along who captured his interest, he was going to spread his wings."

He was absolutely right. But it was *hard* to hear that. So when he said it, I shut him out again. And that's something I'll never forgive myself for.

Because by Christmas 2018 . . . Valdosta was gone.

He was born with congenital heart failure and had a pacemaker. I remember us talking about how he didn't think he'd live to see forty.

He didn't.

His death wrecked me.

Not just because he was gone but because we never made peace. I went to the funeral and stood at the burial site, but I *knew* there was something still lingering between us, something left unsaid.

It wasn't until after my divorce from Legion that I drove out to Valdosta's gravesite to visit him. Just me. And that's when I broke down. I stood there looking at his gravestone, crying and whispering "I'm sorry" over and over again. I never wanted him to leave this world thinking he was just my fallback. I never wanted him to leave here thinking he was just my plan B. I knew intimately what that felt like, and I also knew that's exactly what he thought. That rips me apart to this day. He died thinking, *Here's this woman I really love, and I'm only good enough for her when the other dude lets her down.*

My goodness, that eats at me even now.

The real reason Valdosta and I struggled with working it out? Immaturity. That's it. We were young and bruised from our past traumas. We were trying to figure out who we were while carrying too much emotional baggage. Our fights were petty, in hindsight. Deep down, I believe he was the man I would've married. I think we would've made it. And I *know* I would've been happy. If only I'd listened to my gut.

Seeing clearly means accepting what *is,* not what you *wish* it could be. It means being brave enough to look at the facts and say, *This isn't working. And I deserve better.* And if you're reading this and wondering how to begin trusting your gut again, even after years of not doing so, I want you to know it's possible. You can learn to listen to yourself, to the inner voice that knows what's true even when your heart wants to believe otherwise. And you can start by paying attention to your body.

Your intuition doesn't always speak in words. Sometimes it shows up as a tightness in your chest or maybe a headache that comes on every time that person texts you something that doesn't sit right. With Valdosta, especially during our down times, my gut would just feel like a slight rumble—an irritation that felt like something was missing. But with Dallas and Legion, the physical manifestation of my gut speaking was strong. When Dallas would call or Legion would come home, I would feel nauseous. You know that feeling when your stomach is always in knots? That's how it felt. And I knew it was anxiety because I didn't want to deal with that person. I didn't want to hear whatever it was they were about to say. With Legion, I didn't want to hear whatever lie he was about to come up with.

With Beavis, it wasn't so much a physical sickness as an emotional one. It got to the point that I was just sad all the time. When he came over or called, I'd just be sad, because deep down I knew he didn't want me. And I knew I didn't yet have the strength to walk away. I stayed sad because I didn't have the strength to let go. Even when Beavis told me that he wanted to go out and date other people, I acted like him coming back in between those relationships was a sign that it was meant to be. But my body and my heart were trying to tell me something different. Your body remembers what your mind tries to rationalize, so when your physical self starts reacting, don't dismiss it. Ask it what it's trying to say. The body is often the first to sense what your heart isn't ready to hold.

This whole chapter of my life—the loss of such a beautiful person—disappoints me because it's proof of what happens when immaturity wins. We were both at fault, sure. But I have to believe there could've come a point when we finally looked at each other and said, "Enough is enough. I love you." Because I did love him. But pride and trauma can so easily drown out what your gut is trying to tell you. Your gut is not always yelling, "Stop! Don't go there." Sometimes it's whispering, "You're running out of time. Go love that man."

Valdosta's death has changed the way I deal with men. Now I don't leave anything unsaid, ever. Yes, I try to be mindful, and I try to time my words right. But if I need to say it, I say it. That's why when people ask, "Do you expect closure from Legion?" I tell them no. Because I already said everything I needed to say. I gave myself closure.

Even with Beavis, I rarely listened to my gut. I thought he was so different from Valdosta, but my gut was like, "Girl, no." She told me he didn't see me the way I saw him. That I wasn't his cup of tea. She told me I was setting myself up to be "the good woman he leaves behind." I didn't believe her. I thought if I loved him hard enough, if I behaved, he'd choose me. And what happened? You guessed it. I prolonged the heartbreak.

I know I'm not alone though. Too many women rationalize this in-and-out behavior from their lovers and partners. We say things like, *Well, he knows where home is.* No, ma'am. He knows where his convenience lies. He knows who's going to let him play in their face.

So you can imagine that by the time Legion entered my life, I was tired. I was completely beat up. Not from the heartbreak others had caused but from the pain I had caused myself by ignoring my gut again and again. I wanted to believe I'd learned. That I would tune in to what my gut was saying and act accordingly. But I wouldn't. Not in the beginning, anyway. With Legion, my gut knew something was off, maybe even on our first or second date. It wasn't loud at first. It wasn't saying, "Get the fuck out of here." Not yet. It was more like a hum. An "okay, what is this?" I remember telling my friend, "He talks a lot. He talks more than me." Which, again, isn't necessarily a bad thing—unless that person is talking a lot in order to set the stage for his lies.

So it started off with a "Hmm" and then it turned into a "Wait, what?"

Friends, pay attention to that. Please. It took extreme paranoia to get me to stop ignoring my gut. By the time a whole year had passed and February 2021 came along, my gut was damn near using a bullhorn to warn me.

It was early in our relationship when Legion told me he wanted to buy a house. We weren't married yet, but he claimed to be thinking long-term, and that included a dream home. "We'll do it together," he said. "Let's build a future." My heart perked up. My gut cocked her head. *Girl.*

We went house hunting, and we found one we both loved: brick front, a big backyard, and a kitchen with granite countertops. Legion said he was putting in an offer. The next thing I knew, we were at Home Depot pricing appliances and looking at refrigerator models like we were on HGTV. We sat on sectionals while browsing through furniture stores and argued playfully about area rugs.

My gut said, "This don't feel off to you?"

She whispered again when Legion refused to show me any paperwork. "The offer's in," he said. "We're waiting to hear back." But every time I asked for proof—an email, a realtor's number—he had an excuse. I started to feel like I was watching a play I wasn't cast in. My body tensed up every time he changed the story. I knew something wasn't right, but I wasn't ready to say it out loud.

Instead I started recording audio diaries.

These were just little voice memos on my phone that allowed me to capture what he said, how he said it, and how it made me feel. I needed receipts, not for him but for me. I needed to remember because gaslighting has a way of making you forget your own reality.

I'd sit in the darkness of my closet with the door closed, whispering into my phone like a woman losing her grip. "He said the closing date is next week, but I still haven't seen anything in writing." Or "He took me to a store today to look at washer-dryer combos. Said it was for the new house. I don't believe him."

My gut was practically hoarse by then.

Then there were the women.

I'm not even speaking of the women I caught him sexting with at the end of our marriage. Throughout our relationship, Legion constantly talked about how women were after him. Women from work. Women from the gym. He told me stories about a co-worker who had flirted with him so aggressively that he had to block her on social media. Another woman allegedly showed up at his job unannounced. According to him, she was trying to seduce him in the parking lot.

It was all very dramatic. All very . . . convenient.

Part of me didn't believe him, but another part, the insecure part that had been bruised by Dallas and dismissed by Beavis, wondered if it was true. I'd look in the mirror and wonder, *Am I enough?* Was I attractive enough? Thin enough? Good enough?

That's exactly what Legion wanted—to keep me on edge. He got off on reactions in general, good or bad. It's like he loved watching my face light up about something, knowing that he was going to let me down. And I think he loved to low-key make me compete with women who didn't exist. To keep me just insecure enough to try harder and stay longer.

Again, my gut knew better. But I was still caught in the cycle of denial. I didn't want to admit that I'd fallen for another lie. I wanted to believe that the good parts—the hand-holding, the promises—meant something.

It's hard to explain what it's like to live with someone who lies for sport. You start questioning everything. Every story. Every sigh. Every glance. You don't just lose trust in them; you lose trust in yourself. That's what broke me. Not the lies themselves but how they made me doubt my own judgment.

Facing the truth is the first step to finding freedom though.

Until you do, you'll keep searching for love in all the wrong places. You'll chase illusions and build futures on foundations made of sand. You'll mistake words for actions. You'll ignore your gut, thinking maybe it's just anxiety or that you're being too sensitive. Maybe, maybe, maybe . . .

But no.

Your gut is a divine gift. A holy alarm system. A still, small voice sent by God to keep you safe. And when she speaks, you better listen.

I didn't want to hear her. Because if I had listened, I would've had to admit the dream was a lie. The house wasn't real, and the life we were building stood on quicksand. But once I faced the truth, once I stopped explaining it away, I started to heal. I'm learning to tell the difference now between a nudge from God and a whisper from fear.

Now when my gut says "Hmm," I try not to ignore her. I pause and pray. I investigate.

That's growth.

Next, journal what you feel versus what you're told. Write things down. Use the voice memo feature on your phone and record your thoughts. Seriously. When your partner says one thing but your gut is saying another, document both of them. This is what worked for me. My car and my closet were the two places I loved to record my audio diaries.

In fact, everyone knows that Atlanta has some of the worst traffic in the country. The running joke is, "It takes an hour to get to Atlanta from Atlanta," and let me tell you, it's not an exaggeration. I often found myself sitting for hours in my car, listening to music or an audiobook, or talking on the phone, running my mouth. If I was listening to an audiobook, all too often I would find myself talking back to the characters, as if we were having a full-on conversation. It was this habit that led me to record my first audio diary. My car became my safe place to speak out loud the thoughts I was having. Gone were the teen years of sitting on my bed with a notebook writing "Dear Diary." Recording audio diaries became much easier for me. I could record them anytime and anywhere that was private. There was no better place than my car, driving home. I even began recording on nights when I couldn't sleep. It was my outlet.

But no one was around to hear me as I inched my way down the highways of Atlanta. No one was there to judge the innermost thoughts I had as I cried while talking and sorting my shit out. The audio diaries literally became my therapy sessions. By the time I met Legion, I already had quite a library of audio diaries.

One of the things I quickly figured out from my audio journaling is that there was a lack of quiet in my relationship with Legion. Most days, I felt like the only time I got a chance to breathe and think was when he was at work or sleeping. So I started doing what I'd always done. I began recording my thoughts about the relationship while sitting on the floor in my closet. It was the height of COVID-19, and while he was at work, I would talk about how frustrated I was. How something wasn't adding up. Almost everything was shut down, but I still had this nagging feeling that something was wrong. He would call me every day on his way home from work to talk about his day. Every day, there was a new story about one of his "employees." But again, his words felt off—manufactured, even. I couldn't take it some days, so I would tell him, "Oh, this is my mom calling, I'll see you when you get home." On a few occasions, I would put my phone on airplane mode while he was talking so it looked like I had dropped the call. Then before he got home, I'd go in my closet, sit on the floor, and record my thoughts. The things I questioned, the things I feared—all of it went into those diaries.

Those audio diaries took on a new meaning. They became insurance. I entered a world of pure paranoia. My Google search history probably read like the beginning of a Lifetime movie. "Can my husband get life insurance without my knowledge?" "How to tell if my car has a tracking device?" These were real fears I was fighting in my head. I eventually found myself recording the audio diaries on at least a weekly basis, sometimes even twice a day. It was like my fear had finally lined up with what my gut had been telling me all along, and the roller coaster I was on never seemed to slow down. It was very apparent to me that I was in trouble.

I made a point to tell one person in my life about the audio diaries. My friend Tony was someone I knew well enough that if I told him something but was a bit vague, he wouldn't ask questions. He would just wait until I was ready to talk. I simply sent him a message and said, "I have audio diaries saved in my Google Drive. They are labeled by date." Tony's response was a simple, "Okay, what does that mean?" I explained that I was letting him know "just in case." He didn't ask any further questions, and we didn't discuss it again until a year after the TikTok series came out. I think maybe in hindsight he recognized how important those diaries were for my healing, but at the time, he was fine with just being the one who knew where they were should something have happened to me.

I still have the audio diaries, all arranged by date. I laugh when someone suggests that I release them and put them on social media. I don't think people understand that an audio diary can hold the same weight as a written one. At some point, though, when I am ready, maybe even as part of a healing ritual, I am going to make it a point to pour myself a glass of wine and sit down and delete every single entry I created during the tenure of that relationship. Until then, I will simply suggest that you consider any kind of journaling to help refine your gut-listening skills. Over time, patterns will start to emerge. Your diaries won't just be a record; they will also create distance between your emotions and your reality and allow you to come back to the truth without the fog of manipulation or confusion. I notice this very thing whenever I listen to some of those recordings now. It's so hard to hear that version of myself, to connect with her. It's even harder to hear just how deep she was getting played.

Another way to begin trusting your gut is to ask yourself a simple question: *Am I shrinking?* This is something I wish I'd done at the time. I don't even think I realized that what I was recording was tangible evidence of me making myself small. But please learn from my experience. I know now that in healthy relationships, you expand. You feel seen. You feel safe enough to speak your mind and set your boundaries. If you find yourself making yourself smaller, doing things like holding your tongue to avoid backlash or questioning your value because they say someone better is waiting in the wings, that's not love; that's control. Your gut knows it. Listen.

Silence is also a signal of something being wrong. If you find yourself going quiet more often than not or walking on eggshells around someone, that silence might not be peace; it might be suppression. Ask yourself what's really being muted. Ask your gut what the silence is costing you.

Finally, practice saying no without apology. That's another one I wish I'd done more often. I often used my need for an explanation or a reason as an excuse to say yes to things that didn't feel right. Now I try to give myself permission to say no, whether I can fully explain why or not. That's me trusting my gut. We don't need evidence to honor our inner knowing. If something feels off, it's off. Period. Trust that.

Listening to your gut isn't always easy, especially if you've been manipulated or made to feel crazy. It was so hard for me to hear what was being said to me because my mind was in a constant state of investigation, trying to decipher what was true and what was not. It created too much noise. But once I figured out a way to get still, I was able to hear better. That quiet voice inside us is our God-given gift.

Oh, and another thing: It's way too easy to push away the pink flags. To disregard the little nudges. But inevitably, those pink flags will turn red. And ignoring those pink flags will give you too much time to fall in love. Too much time for the person to gain a stronghold in your mind. By that time, you'll get a message from your gut like the one Whoopi Goldberg's character delivered in the film *Ghost:* "You in danger, girl."

More than anything else I can say, I know that the best way to make a practice of listening to your gut is to first make sure you have spent enough time healing after a relationship ends. Reflection is important. It often gives you the kind of clarity and confidence you'll need to be able to hear clearly the next time you choose to be in a relationship. We all need time to work through our fears. I know I did. I had to sit and think about all the ways my experiences in these relationships have made me hypervigilant. So I can't emphasize enough the importance of not jumping into a new thing so close to the old thing. Sure, healing is not a destination. There is no point up ahead called Healed. It's a process. But at least you'll be a bit further along in that journey when you meet someone you might consider being with.

I know there are some people who will make you believe that being single is the worst thing. That living on your own with no children is the most terrible thing a woman can do. Hell, I was one of those people. That is, until I found out there was absolutely something worse than being single. Are there days when I wish I had someone here? Sure, I'm human. But I also know what it's like to live with someone and have no peace. To become physically ill when I hear the garage door opening because I know some bullshit is about to walk up the stairs.

Listen, there's no foolproof formula to listening to your gut. What worked for me may or may not work for you. I know there are other books that will tell you there is, but I just don't believe it. I believe that we live with the consequences of not listening, and we learn what we can for the next leg of our race. Part of me is changed forever because of what I went through while being married to a pathological liar. How I look at the world, at men, and at relationships is different. I wrestle with the possibility of getting into a new relationship because I'm afraid to find myself in that same place again. To this day, I fight to keep listening to my gut rather than shutting down completely out of fear. A man who comes into my life now will have to know this and be willing to go the extra mile in providing me with both the physical and emotional safety I need. He will have to meet me halfway, be my friend, and do the things I need him to do, because I'm not the same Tareasa I was in 2020 or in 2016.

And that's okay! It's got to be. I know now that I don't need anyone's permission to protect my peace. The more I practice listening to my gut, the clearer my inner voice becomes. So I'm going to let her guide me—not necessarily back to who I was but forward, to who I'm becoming. My gut isn't paranoid. She isn't dramatic. She isn't trying to sabotage my happiness. If anything, she's trying to protect it.

5

I Allowed My Feelings to Drive My Decisions

Feelings are real,
but they don't always lead to truth.

I WOULD SAY THAT EMOTIONS drive me 95 percent of the time. I do not have a good track record of making logical decisions. I just don't. And when it comes to relationships, I have probably stayed in them much longer than I should have based on some emotion I was feeling; fear, love, hope, blah, blah, blah. This is despite my brain always saying, *Come on, Tareasa. Two plus two will always equal four.* Still, my tendency is to let emotions drive choices that should have been grounded in wisdom and faith. I stayed in my marriage because my heart was leading, but without the guidance of my spirit, I ended up following those feelings into heartache.

I know that might sound harsh, like I'm blaming myself for something I didn't know. But I've learned that just because a feeling is real doesn't mean it's true. Feelings aren't facts. And when you don't know how to tell the difference between the two, you end up walking into situations that look like love but feel like chaos. That's what usually happens to me.

I especially let my heart wildly take the lead when I found out I was pregnant two months after meeting and living with Legion.

My cycle was late, and deep down, I already knew. But because I didn't want to get my hopes up, I did the sensible thing and took a test. The moment that second line appeared, my first feeling wasn't excitement. It was panic. *Damn, Tareasa . . . this was fast. You ain't even married yet. On top of that, you're overweight and pushing the age limit.* The incessant negative thoughts just kept coming. It was like my urgency to make my dream of marriage and motherhood come true was fusing with all the lessons about not having children out of wedlock and doing things the right way. And my brain was firing in panic mode. It wasn't that I didn't want a baby. I absolutely did. I wanted a family. I had always dreamed of hearing little feet running down the hallway. Of Saturday mornings with cartoons playing in the background and cereal bowls half full on the kitchen table. So my response to something I had wanted since I was a little girl was strange even to me. There was no part of me that was happy to be pregnant, because, after two months, I didn't know the man I was with (let's be real) and I didn't really trust him. Our arguments had already become too intense and exhausting.

Mostly, though, I was disappointed in myself. I had broken the rules I'd lived by my entire life. *You made it this far, Reesa, and now? You about to be a baby mama. Congratulations. You played yourself.*

When I told Legion I was pregnant, his whole face lit up.

"Are you serious? We're having a baby?!"

He literally jumped off the bed and stared at that test like it was the best news of his life. Legion was over the moon, but I was drowning in fear. He couldn't understand it. "Isn't this what you always wanted?" he asked. I couldn't tell him what I was really thinking—that I carried this heavy, quiet belief that something bad was going to happen. But of course, when you carry that much fear, it starts to show. As a result, we argued constantly in the beginning. He took it personally that I wasn't happy about the baby. I tried to explain how I was feeling. "I'm nervous," I told him. "And I'm plus-size. I'm thirty-five. I don't know how this is going to go. I'm just scared."

There were times when Legion's enthusiasm warmed me. Seconds when I let myself breathe and hope. But then came the doctor's appointment and the confirmation of my pregnancy by the doctor. My due date was January 26, 2021.

And just like that . . . *everything* changed.

My entire focus shifted. Suddenly all I cared about was one thing: having a healthy baby. Okay, two things. A healthy baby and getting married. Yes, you read that right. I was *terrified* to become an unmarried mother, mostly because I knew just how quickly being an unmarried mother could turn into being a single mother if the man didn't act right. Yes, I could hope for a good co-parenting situation if we broke up, but it wasn't guaranteed. I didn't want there to be even a possibility of that. I had been raised by a single mom who worked her ass off to provide for me and still struggled. There were times when I'm sure she was isolated and unsupported. There was no one to team up with when faced with parenting challenges. I promised myself I wouldn't be in that position.

I was also intimately acquainted with the things a child who doesn't have two parental figures misses out on. I grew up looking in the mirror and wondering where some of my features came from. If my father walked by me today, I would not know who he was. His absence has shaped me in ways I am still unraveling. I don't want that for my child, if I can help it. I cannot bring a child into the world to experience that same wound. I wanted my child to have the same last name as me and my husband to show we were a family, which of course doesn't ensure that I wouldn't end up as a single mother, but it felt like the foundation I should aspire to. That was what I had been taught to want. I have enormous respect for women who, either by choice or by circumstance, are single mothers. They are some of the strongest and most resourceful people I know—which is why I was never sure I could handle it. That was my truth. And because of it, I became more obsessed with being married before I gave birth than anything else.

At the time, we were still touring houses, so I found myself imagining nurseries. That's one way I kept my spirits up when the weight of having the baby out of wedlock started to take over. Baby clothes. Car seats. I chose to dream up a vision that could quell my other feelings. I saw it all so clearly: life in a four- or five-bedroom house in Cobb County, Georgia. Me driving a top-of-the-line SUV and my beautiful baby riding in the back seat. I believed I was so close to what I thought was the perfect life for me.

And because I was so close, I told myself that *I'd* be perfect too. No arguments. No drama. No confrontation. I kept things to myself and swallowed every concern and doubt because I thought that if I could just keep things steady, it would protect the life inside me. *Maybe that lie he just told wasn't necessarily a red flag,* I thought. *Maybe I'm just jaded.* I started telling myself that maybe I didn't know what a good man looked like. I was so determined to have this life, and *nothing* was going to mess it up.

Meanwhile, Legion kept coming up with excuses about the house he'd supposedly bid on: why it wasn't working out, why there were delays. Finally, one night, sitting alone in the dark of my closet, I whispered to myself, "He's going to have to lie his way out of this . . . and I'm going to let him." That day still breaks my heart because I know it was the moment I completely compromised myself.

My resolve to simply accept what was happening, to tolerate whatever came as a result of my choice to stay in the relationship, crystallized that following June 2020.

By then, I was in survival mode: pregnant, scared, and doing everything I could not to rock the boat. If Legion said the sky was purple? Fine. It's purple.

I remember one night so clearly. We went to LongHorn Steakhouse to grab dinner. We were still in the middle of COVID, so takeout was our life. Some man in a pickup truck tried to snag the parking spot we were eyeing. It was a small thing, it was but enough to set Legion off.

He jumped out of the car and walked straight up to the man's car window to "have words." My heart damn near stopped. I knew he was about to fight. That's just who Legion was. He was the "I'll beat somebody's ass" type—always talking shit.

I couldn't hear what was said, but from the body language, it didn't seem like it escalated. *Thank God.* Still, walking up to a man's car window like that? In *this* day and age? Not smart.

When he got back in the car, he was full of bravado, talking about, "I'll beat that dude's ass." I just sat there thinking, *Boy, you ain't gonna do shit.* That's always been him—all talk, no execution. But did I say that? Nope. Remember, I'm keeping the boat steady. I just put my hand on his arm and said, "Well, I'm glad it didn't escalate. Let's get our food and go home."

This was my attitude the entire pregnancy: deescalate everything. Smile. Nod. "You're right, honey. You're so tough. You're so big and bad. My man. My man. My man." I chose not to argue. I made decision after decision based on how I felt in the moment instead of anchoring myself in what I knew to be true. I told myself that I was in love, but I was really in fear. I pretended I was protecting my peace, but I was really protecting *his comfort*. In the end, I thought I was doing what good women do by being patient and forgiving. But what I was really doing was betraying myself.

God never told me to lead with my feelings instead of my faith. Yet there I was, doing exactly that. And here's the hard truth I still wrestle with sometimes. There is a part of me that wonders if I deserved what came next. That wonders if, by saying "I'm going to let him," I gave the universe permission to drag me through the mud. *Did I invite all of this in?*

But I didn't. I know that now. I've had to unlearn many things, including that self-blame. I have grace for that version of myself, because she didn't know that God never asked her to shrink to be loved.

Legion was someone who *presented* stability, which has always been the thing I craved the most. It comes from my childhood. We moved around a lot, and I promised myself that when I got grown, I'd plant roots. I'd build something steady. But that desire? It's a blessing and a curse.

Take the Georgia State Patrol, for example. I stayed there for eight years making peanuts. The most I made at that job was $41,000. But I stayed because it was stable. I knew when I was getting paid, and I knew how much. I knew the systems. It was safe. It wasn't until life completely disrupted my routine that I even considered applying for another job. I have a full-time job right now, even though Reesa Teesa blew up my life and I'm traveling all around the world for speaking engagements and opportunities—all because of that same attachment to stability.

Legion had painted a beautiful picture of wanting kids and a family. He had supposedly been with the same company for more than seven years. He said he owned a home in California. He said he was ready to plant roots in Georgia and be near family. It sounded perfect, and it screamed stability. Everything he said made me feel like, *Finally, I can breathe. I can relax. I can build something solid.* That was part of the illusion. I was with someone who got up every day and went to work. That was important to me. But the moment that pregnancy test was positive, all I could think was, *Oh shit!*

I'm sure Legion never really understood the other side of it—the side where I didn't want to be a baby mama. But I didn't want to pressure him into marriage. And that meant I was stuck. Or at least I felt that way. I wanted the baby. I was grateful I was able to get pregnant. But the situation was everything I had spent my life trying to avoid: having a child out of wedlock.

At the time, nobody in my family even knew Legion had moved in with me. But I knew I had to share this news. I sent my mom an email and told her I was pregnant. I also told my aunt and my little cousin.

My aunt came at things from a health standpoint. She'd had my cousin at thirty-six, so she was very encouraging: "Emma came out healthy. Your baby will too. Don't stress. It'll be okay."

My cousin? She was also happy for me.

My mom's response? "I pray y'all talk about marriage." That response was part of the reason I had written to her instead of calling her in the first place. I couldn't bring myself to tell her in person. I didn't have the strength for that. So I wrote her an email. That's always been our thing anyway. When the news is heavy, we write. Then we eventually follow up with phone call.

But even as I wrote that email, I could see the fear lingering all around the edges of my words. Mom eventually came around to being happy for me. But I couldn't even attach to my family's joy. All I could hear was the quiet little voice whispering *This ain't right*. It was the start of it all unraveling.

When I learned that I was miscarrying, it felt like another failure on my part. My cycle of negative self-talk began again, and those feelings of being unworthy, undeserving, and incapable, as false as they were, took over. *I knew something bad was going to happen. I stressed too much. I brought this on.* And I really believed that my body could not hold the anxiety. It was like it said, "Girl, never mind. We ain't even about to do this."

The way the miscarriage happened? Whew . . . let me walk you through it.

I was about nine weeks along when I went in for a routine ultrasound at Kaiser Permanente. I went by myself before work, thinking it would be quick. No big deal.

The ultrasound tech, before she even got started, hit me with "Just so you know, I can't tell you what I see. I'm only allowed to do the ultrasound. Your OB-GYN will go over the results with you." Then she began rubbing the cold jelly-coated wand all along my pelvis.

I still remember asking, "But . . . do you *see* anything?" She just repeated, "I can't tell you."

After the procedure, I went to work and felt fine. Later that day, my OB-GYN called. I'll never forget her words.

"We didn't detect a heartbeat, Tareasa."

I didn't understand what she was saying.

"Okay . . . maybe I'm just too early?"

She paused, then said, "No. The pregnancy isn't viable."

Viable. That's the word that hit me like a freight train. I mean . . . I knew what it *meant.* But still, I wanted her to make it plain. That's when she said, "I'm so sorry, but you are going to have a miscarriage."

After that call, I spoke with the other OB-GYN at the practice, and he laid out my options. "Because of COVID," he explained, "you have three choices. One, you can let it happen naturally. Your body will eventually expel the fetus. Two, you can take a pill to help your body along. Three, you can go to the hospital and have a D&C (dilation and curettage)."

In any other time or season, I would have immediately gotten the D&C, but setting foot in a hospital during COVID was absolutely not an option for me. It felt like everybody was going in but wasn't coming back out.

So that left me with two choices.

I chose the pill.

At the time, I had no idea how much that choice would mess with my head, but Legion and I talked it through. We were already off work around his birthday, so I decided to take the pill that day. We went out to eat like everything was normal, and I took it when we came home.

This isn't a pill you swallow quickly. You place it between your teeth and gums and let it dissolve. The doctor had said, "In about two hours, you'll feel some cramping. Then your body will take care of the rest."

What he *should've* said was, "In about two hours, it's going to feel like your insides are trying to kill you."

It was the most excruciating shit I've ever been through.

I spent the entire night in the bathroom, pacing, crying, and hunched over in pain. Legion tried to be supportive. He rubbed my back and was saying all the right things, but it was horrible.

I feel for *any* woman who has to take that pill option. Looking back, I'm sure it also would've been hard, but I think letting it happen naturally would have been better for me. Because the worst part, the part that tormented me for weeks, was the doubt.

What if they were wrong?

What if "no heartbeat" didn't mean no life? What if, had I waited, they would've discovered, "Oops, the heartbeat's there after all! You're perfectly pregnant. Everything's fine. Our bad"? That thought ate me alive for weeks, because as much as I hated the idea of being pregnant and not married, as much as I struggled with feeling happy about the circumstances in which the child was being brought into the world, the last thing I ever wanted was to lose my baby.

To make matters worse? The pill didn't even fully work.

Two weeks later, I went back for another ultrasound. That's when they told me that everything hadn't passed. I'd have to go to the hospital for a D&C anyway.

Thankfully the D&C procedure wasn't invasive at all. Recovery should've only taken thirty to forty-five minutes. Unfortunately, I was in the recovery room for three hours. Why, you ask? Well, it was because I was waiting for Legion to come and get me. He was late.

I get that my miscarriage was *not* like those stories you hear from women who rush to the bathroom in shock, bleeding everywhere. Mine started in that cold, dark ultrasound room with a technician who couldn't tell me anything, and later two little words: *not viable.*

I didn't experience the emotional kind of pain you see in the eyes of grieving mothers on television. Not at first, anyway. That night in the bathroom was 95 percent blinding, excruciating physical pain. It was so bad that I couldn't even process the fact that I was losing a baby. The emotional part came later. It wasn't until I was home alone on bed rest after the D&C that the grief snuck in. And it settled in for the long haul.

It wasn't just the baby I grieved either. It was the version of myself that had believed I could manufacture feelings and build a life on them. The part of me that believed if I just prayed long enough and stayed quiet enough, everything would work out. I was grieving her too, because clearly that wasn't true.

Ironically, during this recovery time, Legion cared for me in a way I think every woman deserves. It's wild to say considering how things turned out, but in those first few days after I was in the hospital, he briefly became the partner I'd wanted all along. I could barely walk. I couldn't change my clothes or bathe myself. And he did all of it, with no attitude or complaints. For a minute, I thought, *Oh, this is what a good man looks like when life breaks you down.* He was selfless and gentle—exactly what I needed. And so, once again, I chose to forget about all the lies.

The miscarriage made me cleave to Legion not because I suddenly fell deeper in love but because I was grateful that he didn't leave me when my body failed. And I did feel like my body had let me down, which in my mind meant that I'd let him down too. So instead of the miscarriage being the moment I let him go, it became the moment I held on tighter.

I half expected him to say, "Well, damn, you can't give me a kid . . . I'm out." But he didn't. And because he didn't leave, I didn't leave either. It was me saying, "Thank you for not abandoning me because I lost a baby."

As for his grief, I didn't really *see* it. Not beyond what he told me. Sure, he said he was sad, and I believe he actually was. For all the lies and all the nonsense, I believe there was a broken part of him that genuinely wanted the family, the kids, the wife—the picture-perfect life.

But I was shattered. I questioned my worth during those months afterward, and I definitely felt like less of a woman. And yes, I blamed myself. On some level, I think Legion blamed me too. Nevertheless, that was my out. That was the moment I should've walked away. I didn't know just how much not doing so would cost me.

People often forget that fear is an emotion too. And my fear of being single, of running out of time to have a baby, and of being a single mom had me making excuses for foolishness. It had me doing the mental *la, la, la,* blocking out every red flag, because what if this was my last chance? Then, after my miscarriage, instead of leaving like I could have, I pushed myself even deeper into survival mode. *The bills have to get paid. I can't afford to think about leaving.* It was still fear; it just came from a different angle.

The truth is, there must be a happy medium, a balance, between logic and emotion. You can't live life by only being logical with no heart. But living off pure emotion is dangerous too. Emotions will have you making excuses for messes you'd never tolerate if you were thinking straight. In fact, when you strip the emotions away, so many situations become black and white. Suddenly it's easy to say, *I'm out. I'm done.*

This is probably why I won't entertain a relationship unless it starts with a friendship now. People act like that's obvious, but how many of us jump into relationships with folks we weren't friends with to start? In that situation, there's no foundation. No logic. All emotions. *Passion,* we call it. But really it's fear. Or loneliness. Or insecurity. In friendship, there's space. There's logic. We argue, but I don't spiral thinking my friend is gone for good because we fought over where to eat. So now if someone says, "Hey, Reesa, wanna meet a guy? Want to go on a blind date?" My answer is emphatic: "No!"

That's because I know myself better now. I know I have an anxious attachment style. If you argue with me, my mind goes straight to *You're going to block or ghost me. I'll never hear from you again.* But if someone says, "Hey, Reesa, wanna meet up and hang out with a group of single friends?" That's cool. In friendship, there's room to breathe. There's grace for imperfections. That has to be the foundation of any relationship I have going forward.

Listen, I know better than anybody that feelings change with the wind. They respond to pressure, and sometimes they even mislead us. Our emotions are like the weather: real, present, and important but not permanent. So don't stake your life on them. Balance them with logic and commitment.

Like many of us, I used to think that *follow your heart* was the best advice anyone could give. There *is* some good in that. But sometimes the desires of our hearts are rooted in trauma. Sometimes we have absorbed the messages of society or of the generations before us that did not have the resources and options we do now. Sometimes our hearts are rooted in poor attachment styles. I think it's important to ask ourselves, *What are my emotions anchored to?* I have friends who have a fear of abandonment. They believe everyone is trying to leave them. There are others who have been taught, sometimes inadvertently, that their voice doesn't matter in the grand scheme of things. It reminds me of the *children should be seen and not heard* teachings of my childhood. There are consequences for that kind of indoctrination. And then there are people like me who often mistake attention for affection. We run full speed ahead when someone shows us any kind of attention, letting our longings lead us into disappointment.

I have a new mantra now though: *Follow your heart only when it's in alignment with your spirit.* Because your spirit is where wisdom lives. God will not guide you into things that will destroy you. Yes, that miscarriage broke something in me, but it also birthed something new. It made me pay attention to how much I had abandoned myself. It made me ask why I thought "rocking the boat" meant I couldn't be loved well. It's important to remember that feelings and emotions are often shaped by what we believe—about ourselves, about love. And those beliefs will ultimately shape our decisions. Our emotions are human, but if we don't learn to put them in their proper place, they will run our lives; they will run us right into decisions that contradict the very things we say we believe. Too many times, I've mistaken passion for true affection based on an adrenaline rush. I've mistaken chemistry for character. Yet I invite us all to treat our emotions like indicators and not instructions. Examine them. Hold them up to the light. And then lovingly ask, *Is this true? Is this real? Or is this something else? Is this love, or is it longing?* In my case, I need to ask myself, *Is this my fear talking?*

If you're saying yes to something when your spirit is screaming no, I encourage you to take that in. Because God doesn't speak in confusion and doesn't lead through fear. He doesn't ask you to carry something that's breaking you down just to prove your strength. He does ask you to trust Him though.

Again, I'm not suggesting you shut off your emotions and stop feeling at all. Oh no, we need that part of us! Emotions are just not meant to drive the car. They're passengers. Put wisdom behind the wheel. Let truth guide you, not just with what feels good in the moment but with what aligns with the life you know you've been called to. You are allowed to feel, but you are also allowed to *question* those feelings. You are allowed to love, but you are also allowed to *walk away* when love doesn't look like safety or respect. And you are allowed to change course, not just after heartbreak but now. Today. While your heart is still healing. While your spirit is still learning how to discern. I know I am.

6

I Second-Guessed Myself

Trusting yourself is an act of courage.

FIVE WORDS HAVE CAUSED ME more trouble than just about anything else in my romantic relationships: *What if I am wrong?* I cannot tell you how many times I've asked myself that question. For every argument my brain made about a relationship, my heart would whisper, *But what if I am wrong?* It was exhausting. I have *what-if*ed myself into staying in some deeply toxic situations, all because I feared being wrong and ending up alone.

There's something particularly cruel about being in a relationship that makes you feel like you can't trust yourself or your *own mind.* I didn't get there overnight, but brick by brick, Legion chipped away at my confidence until I couldn't tell the difference between intuition and insecurity. I know now that it was intentional. He preferred this form of abuse over putting his hands on me.

In fact, the only time Legion tried to physically intimidate me was when he punched a hole in the wall. Sure, he was always talking about how he was going to beat someone's ass or explaining why he "almost" got into a fight. He was absolutely obsessed with fighting Beavis, even though he didn't know anything about the man and had never met him. He just knew that I was in love with him once, and he hated that fact. But Legion never put his hands on me. In hindsight, what he *did* do felt more insidious and what I would classify as emotional abuse.

Legion's MO was to do things to get a reaction out of me. It was the weirdest thing. One time he went to the ends of the earth just to see how I would react to a stranger coming to my home.

The whole thing started in 2021 when I was at the nail salon one day. Legion texted me just as I was getting in the chair for a pedicure.

LEGION: Someone just came to the house looking for you.

What?! I was stunned. I didn't usually have uninvited guests—and especially not in the middle of the pandemic.

I'd driven Legion's car to the salon, so mine was parked in the garage. If someone had pulled into the driveway, it would have looked like no one was there.

"Well, who was it?" I texted back.

LEGION: I don't know, it was a black Dodge Charger. They backed in and got out the car. When I opened the door, I said, "Can I help you?" And they said, "I'm looking for Tareasa."

What in the world?

ME: Was it a man or a woman?

LEGION: It was a man.

As I was reading these texts, I was sitting in the chair, racking my brain, trying to figure out who it could have been. At the time, we didn't have any security cameras outside, so there was no way for me to go look at any footage. Legion knew that too.

ME: Well, what did he look like?

That's when things got vague.

LEGION: I mean, he was shorter than me.

Legion is 6'4", so that wasn't telling me much.

ME: Well, was he skinny, fat?"

LEGION: Umm, he was medium build.

Again, very vague.

I was still at the salon, but I was shooting off all these questions via text because I really wanted to know who it was. Meanwhile, Legion's responses went back and forth between being vague and being accusing.

LEGION: I'm not worried about it. Why are you worried about it? The fact that you're stressing, trying to figure out who this person is, is real suspicious to me.

See? I was way more concerned with my safety. All I kept thinking was *Oh my God, who was that? Why are they coming to my house?*

So I wrapped up my pedicure and rushed home. As soon as I

arrived, I pummeled him with questions about what this person looked like and what they had said. Legion interpreted this as me thinking the person was someone I had been seeing. "No, no, no," I said. "The last guy I dated before you was more than a year ago."

Legion was not happy that I was stressing over this. He clearly didn't think I'd have the reaction I did, so in a way, whatever he was trying to do was backfiring epically.

"Listen, I have to address whoever this was, because it's not okay for them to stroll up to my house. We are living in dangerous times."

"But I live here. They ain't going to do nothing." *There he goes. Ready to fight.*

That still didn't make it okay. Something wasn't making sense to me.

Eventually, he went with his old standby. "I bet you it was that nigga Beavis."

"What?! No, it wasn't."

"I bet it was. How you know it wasn't? So you must still be talking to him."

We were now exactly where he wanted this conversation to go.

"You know what? Don't even worry about it," I said. "I'll talk to Renee."

Renee was my neighbor, and she had a doorbell camera. That's when he started to get nervous. He sat up. "Why do you need to talk to her? I told you I handled it."

We know by now how this eventually went, right? I texted Renee and asked her to check her camera footage to see if a car had pulled up to my house that day. Of course, she didn't see anything. My intuition had been screaming all along at me that nobody had come, but my brain couldn't wrap itself around the reason why Legion would have claimed that in the first place. Renee just confirmed what I already knew.

Second-guessing myself had become a pattern in our relationship, but this was the very first time I felt the intensity of it. When people hear this story, so many of them say, "Girl, when he lied about the first house, you should have known," but it wasn't until this story that I honestly asked myself, *What the fuck am I dealing with?* I think it's because it felt so unnecessary. When it came to the house he had lied about in Douglasville, I thought there had to be a reason. Maybe he had some shame around his ability to provide. I could rationalize to myself that he'd gotten into a situation where a lie he told because he wanted to make me happy had spiraled out of control. But this time, it felt like a strange game. There was no reason to manufacture this story in this way.

For example, when we were looking for homes, he'd take me to see a house just to enjoy how excited I'd get over the kitchen design or the great room layout or the garage space. He'd watch with amusement as I talked about wanting the primary bedroom on the same level as the other bedrooms or one day going to London and staying at the Savoy. I suppose it would have been okay if it was just my positive reactions feeding him. But it wasn't. While I don't think he necessarily enjoyed Angry Tareasa, there seemed to be a part of him that wanted to invoke a negative reaction in me to prove some point or narrative he'd made up in his mind. Yes, he got off on seeing me light up, but in a weird way, he also got his dopamine hit from seeing me upset—like watching my disappointment was some kind of entertainment.

To be honest, I think him enjoying my excitement was the worst form of manipulation, and I think it was all part of his game. He wasn't excited to see me happy just because I was his girlfriend or wife and he wanted me to have all the things. He was excited to see me happy because he knew full well that he wasn't going to follow through on any of it. His joy likely came from the anticipation of my future disappointment. It was his way of putting me in my place—controlling the emotional temperature in the relationship. As long as *he* dictated when I could be happy, when I could be hopeful, and when I could feel loved, he stayed in power.

But again, that *What if I'm wrong?* is powerful. I started to make up scenarios in my mind in which Renee's camera hadn't caught it all. Or maybe she had just missed that part. Second-guessing myself was more than just not listening to my gut and the love-hate relationship I have with it. It went a step further. This was me hearing my gut and considering what it was saying but also hearing the myriad other very reasonable possibilities that could make what was happening make sense. My gut was saying Legion was lying, and I agreed that it was possible he was. But I also believed there could be a logical explanation or even a reason for the lie that would make me lean toward compassion rather than anger in my response.

Please understand that I had never met anyone else like Legion before. Sure, I knew people lied. Everyone does a white lie here and there. "Does this make me look fat?" someone will ask. A significant other might answer, "Nah, you look good." But this was entirely different. With these kinds of lies, there's enough room, enough ambiguity, for there to be a constant fight between my brain and my heart. My brain was saying, "But Tareasa, why would he lie about that? Why would he lie about somebody coming to the house? There is no reason someone in their right mind would make that up." And my heart would say, "He loves you, girl. He wouldn't make up something that insignificant." Of course, my intuition was saying, "Something isn't right. You know it. You feel it." It was a three-way fight between my intuition, my heart, and my brain. They were never on the same page.

I kept asking myself, *What if I break up with him and then find out I'm wrong? What if he's not lying—because who lies about being able to buy a house when I actually saw and held the paperwork? Who lies about someone coming to the house?* Then there was the bigger question, the one that used all my previous relationship pain to turn the narrative on me: *Are you that messed up that you can't see a loving man when he is in front of you?* That's what manipulation does, though. It clouds your clarity and convinces you that the problem is *you*. But I wasn't crazy; I was just being conditioned to accept confusion as a normal feeling. This same confusion is what messed with my ability to really pay attention to my gut.

I eventually got to a place where I chose to say, "What can you prove?" That was my barometer for what was true or not. When it came to the house, he'd shown me the preapproval letter, so I knew he at least had the credit to get the mortgage. Every time my intuition threw up a red flag, my brain said, *But what if you're wrong? Don't just go off what he's saying; look at what you have physically seen. You've seen him log in to his phone and show you an account that has $15,000 in there, so you know he has money. You know the bills are getting paid, because he's sending you the money to pay them.* And that was true—no bill payments were ever late.

My brain could never have comprehended that someone would go so far as fabricating their own mortgage preapproval letter or obtaining a screenshot of a bank account balance that wasn't theirs. So even my decision to judge whether he was telling the truth based on what I could "prove" didn't work in the end. But this provability was what kept me going back and forth in my mind.

Then my heart would jump in and add fuel to the fire. It co-signed my brain and its logic with my emotional attachment. I wanted to believe him. I wanted it to make sense. And that's what our hearts do. They find and add meaning to what we see. My heart wanted the things Legion said to be true, so it linked arms with my brain to double-team my intuition. "Maybe you're just jaded," they'd say to me. My brain was using the knowledge of my past experiences against me, and my heart was using my present desires.

One of the many things I wish I'd been better at during this season of my life was talking to my family and friends about the problems I was having with Legion. In fact, I'm absolutely guilty of painting a picture that suggested things weren't perfect but that they also weren't *that* bad. None of my friends would have said during this time, "Oh child, she's really going through it with him." This was because I shared only enough honesty to keep people calm. When it came to my family, they knew about my miscarriage. They knew I had to go to the hospital. What they didn't know was that Legion wasn't going to take me there. He claimed he had a business meeting at that time. They didn't know the true ugliness of our relationship until the day I kicked him out. Even then, I was guarded. As crazy as this sounds, the fifty-part TikTok series was a revelation for them. They had *some* idea of what had happened, but they did not know the full scope until then. My mother definitely didn't.

Part of why I kept so much to myself was that I imagined the questions: *How did you not know? Why didn't you talk to us?* Especially because I had moved so fast with him. The truth is, I didn't want the *I told you so*. And let the record show, *I told you so* isn't always spoken aloud. Sometimes it's communicated in a look. Sometimes it's a quiet "bless your heart," as they say in the South. It can be the unspoken judgment from people who love you. *How did you miss this? How did you not see the red flags? Why didn't you say something?* I wasn't ready to face that. In truth, it wasn't just that I was not ready to face them; I also wasn't ready to face myself. No one can ask me a question I haven't already asked myself. No one could call me a word that I hadn't already called myself. I just wasn't ready to face the ugliness of everything.

With friends, I was more indirect. I'd float scenarios without context. I asked one friend, "When you bought a house, did you have to show proof of funds before or after the offer?" But I never laid out the full picture.

The only person I spoke to before getting married was my best friend, Shawn. I asked her, "What do you think about Legion? What's your vibe?" She paused and said, "He seems like a nice guy, but there's something . . ."

I agreed immediately. "Yeah. There's something. I can't put my finger on it."

Still I went ahead and married him.

People often ask me, "Why didn't you talk to your family? Why didn't you talk to your friends?" As I've mentioned, I really didn't want to hear anything negative. I believed and hoped that it was my turn. This just wasn't how I wanted it to look. I wanted the bridal shower, the bachelorette party, and all the other first-time moments. And I was close to having them—close enough that I didn't want anyone saying, "Maybe this isn't your season." Deep down, though, I knew that if I told the truth, I might have to acknowledge that it really *wasn't* my turn after all.

That was too hard to face.

Maybe if I had been vulnerable with the people I trusted most, there might have been some judgment, but there also might have been intervention. It might have saved me from going too far. And by *too far,* I mean marriage. It might have spared me the paperwork, the unraveling, and the aftermath. Maybe I still would've been hardheaded and said, "Y'all don't know what you're talking about. I love him. He loves me." Who knows? What I do know is that my embarrassment ran deep, especially with the people closest to me. I wanted to say, "I promise you, I'm not this dumb." And yet I had to confront the truth: I had reached a level of desperation I didn't want to admit to.

I distinctly remember sitting on my closet floor to make another audio diary and praying. "Okay, God, I'm not stupid, but what am I missing? I know what I saw, but there's a piece missing somewhere. I don't want to continue accusing him if he's not lying, but I need these blanks filled stat!" That's how intense my prayers had become at one point. It was like I'd returned to what I saw growing up in the church and in my grandmother's closet. And I have to admit that crying out for help ultimately drew me closer to God and eventually gave me clarity as I continued to hem and haw about what was going on.

ANOTHER ONE OF THE ARGUMENTS Legion and I had—one that caused me to second-guess myself even more—was around the third house we'd found. We were working with an agent named Scott, who told us that the sellers wanted to see proof of funds because Legion had put in an all-cash offer. Legion said, "I will show them the proof of funds when they accept the offer." His reasoning was that he didn't want them to start a bidding war with other buyers. After some discussion back and forth, it became a stalemate, and we ultimately didn't get the house.

I asked the people in my life if that made sense. My mom said, "Well, I kind of understand it, because I wouldn't want to open up my bank statement either if they didn't accept my offer." But there were several other people in my life who said, "No, your proof of funds should have gone out with the offer. It's not done after the fact." But that lack of clarity just added to my confusion. So, leading with my heart, I decided to side with Legion. I was already unfamiliar with the homebuying process, so that felt easier than fighting him on it.

To be fair, Legion wasn't the first man to cause me to second-guess myself. Clearly, I've been in other relationships where my voice got smaller and smaller until I barely recognized myself. I learned how to shrink to make others comfortable because it felt like I was being mature, understanding, even godly. But really, I was being silenced. And worse? I was participating in my own silencing. Legion just took it to another level.

One of the ways I could have answered that incessant *What if I'm wrong?* in my head would have been to play it all the way out. Was being wrong that bad? If I found out later that Legion had been telling the truth, couldn't I just apologize? Maybe he would bend over backward to give me more evidence and fight for me. But that's the thing: Deep down, I didn't think he would fight for me. I knew he wouldn't. So I believed that, if I was wrong, I would be giving up on my dream of a family. If I was wrong, I would have lost a good man. If I was wrong, that meant I was really fucked up. Remember, it was all about marriage for me. I believed I was on my way to my happily ever after, so I thought I had to be careful not to ruin it.

That *what if* gets us in trouble so much. It keeps us in situations we shouldn't be in and hides the real questions we should be asking ourselves, like, *What can I live with?*—or, even better, *What if I'm right?* I wish I would have asked myself *that* just one good time. That question could have opened a path that led me to healing so much sooner. At the very least, I would've saved myself the government paperwork. I didn't ask myself this question until April 2021, when things had gone downhill quickly. But I'm glad I eventually did. Because that simple question of *What if I'm right?* led to other necessary reflections. *What if I'm not crazy? What if, in fact, I am picking up on Legion's foolishness much faster than he's expecting, or he's hoping I'm stupid or desperate enough to turn a blind eye?* And most of all: *What does this mean for my reality? Can I live with this?* Because some of it is truly about which version of this relationship you can live with. Can you live with a version where your spouse lies every now and then, manipulates you here and there, and you deal with that for four years or more? Or is there a version where you say to yourself, *I cannot do this. I cannot be in this constant state of paranoia and uncertainty*?

I have to say, my paranoia was bad—*really* bad. But strangely, I'm not embarrassed by it. If anything, remembering it makes me emotional. I was absolutely terrified. Genuinely scared. My mind kept spiraling around one question: *What the hell is going on?*

The paranoia manifested in very specific ways. First I became convinced that Legion had taken out a life insurance policy on me. He had access to my Social Security number because it was on our marriage license, and my Social Security card lived in my wallet. I kept thinking, *If he wanted to, he could take my Social, fill out paperwork, and get a policy while I'm asleep.* I imagined how far this could go—how something could happen to me, and no one would ever suspect foul play. It could look like I had died of natural causes. I imagined my story ending up on the Investigation Discovery channel and my family and friends being interviewed and talking about how great I *was*.

Second, I was certain he'd put a tracker on my car. I really believed that. This wasn't because I was binge-watching true crime shows or watching *Snapped* or *Fatal Attraction*. This fear came from exhaustion. From not sleeping. From my nervous system being completely shot.

The only place I felt truly safe was in my office at Georgia State Patrol. And when I say "safe," I mean *nobody can reach you, nobody can touch you, nobody can just show up*. At work, the tracker would show I was inside the building, but he couldn't just drive up and find me. He would have had to get through a security gate, and someone would have to call me first. That was the only place where my body finally believed everything was okay. The only place where I could exhale. Imagine staying in your office late, not because of your workload or a special project but because you were so messed up that you believed it was the safe and quiet space you craved.

Once again, I couldn't bring myself to tell my family or friends. I knew that if I told Shawn, she would have called *everyone*. I love her, but I know her. She isn't the type to be silent when a friend is in trouble. She would've been like, "What the hell is going on? Why are you telling me about some secret diaries?" And I wasn't ready for that kind of exposure.

It was such a stagnant time in my life. I was stuck. Even my prayers felt stale. The best way I can describe it is the feeling of being so frustrated that you're on the verge of tears because you know you're missing something, but you can't see it. I wasn't sleeping. I wasn't thinking clearly. I certainly wasn't forming a plan.

And yet I believe that God was still trying to speak to me through all of it. I imagine Him saying, "She can't hear me. She's not listening. Everything I'm sending her way she can't hear because fear has twisted her thinking. Chaos and turmoil have taken over. The enemy is having a field day in her mind and spirit. So I'm going to create quiet—real quiet—so she can finally hear my voice."

God never stopped speaking to me. I just wasn't listening. All I could hear was my own thoughts.

By the time I did ask myself if I could live this way, the answer was clear as day: *Hell no, I cannot stay with this person.* But then I was faced with an even more painful possibility: *What if God didn't allow this relationship to fall apart and had given me exactly what I thought I wanted because I was so deep in my feelings about being too old to have children or having to wait too long for a husband?* That question haunts me, but it also reminds me that some of my unanswered prayers were actually God protecting me.

I'm thankful that my spirit never stopped nudging me, even when I ignored it. Even when I was drowning in doubt and couldn't hear anything but Legion's voice, God was still whispering: "Come back to yourself. Trust me."

Whew! That was so hard for me.

Most of us who stay just a little too long in bad relationships don't leave until the pain of staying is greater than the pain of leaving. As our elders used to say, "When you get sick and tired, truly sick and tired, you'll finally get up and go." That was me unfortunately. And I paid a price for that. When we stay with a person even while knowing that something isn't adding up, the mental games can end up driving us up a wall. It's too easy to end up not being an authentic version of yourself because you're constantly asking yourself, *What is going on?* And even when you do leave, trusting yourself feels out of the question.

We can't forget how the trauma of constantly second-guessing ourselves can impact our future. I've bought a house on my own now, but I took my realtor through it because I had so much PTSD from those experiences with Legion. At every point in the process, I was terrified of losing the home I wanted. With every phone call I received from my agent, I was afraid that home was going to be taken away from me. It got to the point when she finally said, "Tareasa, I did not realize the circus this man put you through. You don't have to worry about that anymore."

Trusting yourself after years of second-guessing is hard. Nowadays I'm definitely *better* at trusting myself when it comes to my relationships with men, but I haven't ventured back out there as much because of the uncertainty I still have around whether the trust I claim for myself can hold up against my desire for love and companionship. I know now that being single isn't a dirty word, but I still don't particularly like it. However, I also don't want to go through the hell I went through ever again. If that's the alternative, then being single ain't that bad. But I fear meeting someone and forgetting all the shit I went through because they make me feel like Christmas Eve, butterflies and all. I'm afraid that I will quickly jump back into the train of thought of *marriage, marriage, marriage, kid, kid, kid.*

I suppose I don't trust that my mentality won't revert to the familiar at the first sign of true attention and affection. No, I don't think I'm as desperate to get married as I was at thirty-five, because now I know what that's like. The shit is hard. But I do feel worried that I could be so enamored by the possibility that I would forget the pain I experienced. I don't want to forget. I know psychologists will break this down as a classic trauma response, and I'm good with that. I don't want to forget the pain because I don't want to ever repeat it. It just is what it is.

But I am trying to trust myself more, and I think that's all we can ask of ourselves. One of the things I try to do often is check in with my intuition. Especially since I understand its dynamic now with my brain and heart. My intuition is petty, for sure. She's like, "Bitch, I tried to tell you, you ain't listen. Bet you're going to listen now." And I do. I listen closely and examine when I feel something is not right.

Some people reading this might be thinking, *Can't you be in a relationship and also be mindful of what you went through, so it doesn't happen again?* I suppose I could. But I said in the beginning of this book that I'm a work in progress, and I meant that. I don't know that I'm in a place where I can embrace the fullness of love and companionship while simultaneously remembering the emotional and mental gymnastics I put myself through when I constantly second-guessed myself. I'm not sure if old Tareasa and all her *my man, my man, my man* shenanigans won't show up. So I have to be careful. Maybe when the longing for marriage and children becomes less important than other things I want to accomplish, I will feel more free to dive into a relationship with my eyes wide open. But at this writing, I'm not there yet. There's still some grief. I've not quite arrived at acceptance, but I am in a place where I'm trying my hardest to make peace. I'm making peace with little Reesa, who thought that by forty she was going to have achieved a particular vision for her life that has not yet happened. I did not see the life I have now. I didn't see any of this coming. And that is probably the most honest thing I can say.

If you had said to me at thirty-four, "Honey, there's worse things than being single," I would've believed you out of respect, but I wouldn't have truly known that to be true the way I know it now. Like many other women and men, I've had to learn that lesson from experience. I'm not pressed for marriage because I know what it's like to have been married to the wrong person, and that's a different type of hell. Are there some people who choose something else? Who make peace with their hellish marriages? Sure. I was certainly on that track. But I know now that better awaits me. And better awaits you too.

So many of our mothers and grandmothers chose hellish marriages out of necessity rather than love. Because the world wasn't set up for their thriving as single people and single parents. But I live in a generation when it's not necessary for me to be afraid to go home, because I can buy my own house without the signature of a man. I don't have to be married and be terrified that I wouldn't be able to survive without him. I'm grateful for that freedom.

That said, please don't hear this as a celebration of divorce. Divorce—even though it was just a six-month marriage, even though it was uncontested and we had no children—was one of the ugliest, most emotional things I've been through. It's still a form of grief. When I got my divorce papers, I sat on the steps inside that townhouse and I wept. I mean a deep, from-the-soul kind of weeping. I felt like a complete idiot and a failure. I don't wish that experience on anyone.

If you've ever found yourself questioning your memory and your instincts, know that you're not alone. I gave the loudest microphone in my life to someone who only wanted to drown out my voice, and for a long time, I didn't even realize it was happening. But I know now that I (and you) deserve to take up all the space we want.

I encourage every one of us to get to the point where we have the fortitude to sort through all the confusing and competing voices inside and stand on business when something is not worth our time—no matter how much we desire what we think is being offered. As much as I wanted to be married and have kids, I didn't have to put up with what I did. And going forward, I'm not willing to settle for less than I deserve. Being in love, being in a relationship, is not supposed to be that hard and painful, especially early on. Will there be challenges? Absolutely. But there's a difference between conflict and straight-up confusion. And my God is not the author of confusion. The former can be worked through; the latter is often a symptom of something deeper and more problematic.

The first couple of years in any relationship should be foundational, in that you and your partner are building upon what you know about each other and, in this season, you are vibing in that space. When that happens, I won't have to worry about whether someone said that thing to me because it was just something I wanted to hear, and he actually has some nefarious agenda on the back end. I won't have to go back and forth with myself over whether it is true or not. I will know without a shadow of doubt that he is feeling me and that he's being honest in his words and his actions.

When you find yourself second-guessing everything, try to get still so you can hear beyond your brain and heart. That inner knowing is still in you; it just might be buried under years of manipulation and fear. It's waiting to be trusted again—so make space to hear yourself think. That might mean journaling or creating audio diaries like I did. It might be turning off your phone and going on long walks. Whatever it is, try to get still so you can move from *What if I'm wrong?* and *What can I prove?* to *What if I'm right? What if God is showing me something here?*

Also, pay attention to patterns. Not just in your partner—that's a given—but in yourself. Your body knows when you're ignoring something or making an excuse for someone else's bad behavior.

Let those feelings that show up be your data. Then, once you are aware of those patterns, practice rebuilding your self-trust by making smaller, less consequential decisions. Choose yourself when it comes to little things like who you're going to call back or what you are going to say. Then observe how you feel afterward. Do you feel calm? At peace? Welp, that just might be your intuition saying, *Yes, more of that.* If you're someone who finds strength in faith, remind yourself that your intuition is often the first way God speaks to you. Discernment is not something you have to earn. You were born with it. I grew up hearing people talking very casually about trusting God, and yes, for me that's foundational. But trusting God also means trusting the discernment He put inside you. Your intuition is not being too emotional. You are not overthinking it. Your boundaries are sacred and God-given. And if someone makes you feel like you're in a constant state of confusion and implies that this is what it means to be in a relationship, they are wrong. That's not love; that's control. And it will be an act of courage to release those feelings.

7

I Chose the Devil I Know Because I Didn't Know My Worth

Familiarity isn't worth the price of your peace.

HAVE YOU HEARD THE SAYING "The best way to get over someone is to get under a new someone"? Well, I am guilty of practicing that. However, in my case, it was the same someone.

Now don't judge me before I explain.

Back in 2017, there was a guy I started dealing with . . . let's call him Washington Monument (WM) . . . because *if you know, you know.* WM was the kind of guy you could call when your relationship ended and you needed your physical needs fulfilled. Some people might call him my "maintenance man" or another "situationship." He was my little secret, and that made our encounters that much more alluring. There were times when I was in the same room with him and mutual friends, and you would never have known he was the one blowing my back out.

WM and I had an understanding though. When I was in a relationship, I was not going to be dealing with him, and vice versa. Did he still call periodically to get a status update? Sure. Once I met Legion and saw that marriage was possible, I decided I wasn't going to talk to anyone who could derail me from that goal, and I cut off communication with WM entirely. It was a bit easier to do since it was the middle of COVID, but I don't think WM was too happy about it. It meant our creeping had finally come to an end.

The thing is, I was totally clear that there was no future whatsoever with WM. I knew that the worst thing I could do was catch feelings for the "maintenance man." So I didn't. But I did care about him. Over the years, he'd helped me out financially when I needed money for groceries or gas and had been as good of a friend as he could be. But I knew his capacity was limited. I was never going to grow old with him. He was like that favorite sweater you have in the back of the drawer: cozy and familiar. And what we were doing was probably the most consistent thing in my life. He was the man who could always make me feel good—the devil I knew.

To be fair, though, I never thought of WM as a "devil." I considered him more like medicine. But I never acknowledged that I might have been a bit addicted to the feeling his medicine gave me. If I was involved with someone, WM simply became an afterthought. But when my heart got broken, I turned right back to him.

It has really only dawned on me while writing this book that this was my pattern. Meet John Doe. Date John Doe. Break up with John Doe. Call my friend WM to tide me over until I meet someone else. Meet Henry. Date Henry. Leave Henry. Call my friend WM to tide me over until I meet someone else. It's almost as if, subconsciously, I always knew he'd be there, just a phone call or a text away. I turned to that man so many times that it was second nature to reach out whenever life wasn't going well and I needed my "medicine."

When I was going through my divorce, of course I turned to WM. I distinctly remember how awful I felt during that season. There was finally a moment when it crystallized that everything Legion had said was a lie, and it tore me up inside. So for a while afterward, I had the mentality of *Okay, I'm going to call WM, because I don't want to feel anything, and he specializes in exactly that.* It didn't help that I was ending a marriage in which the sex had stopped. We'd gotten married in January, and by the beginning of March, right before I found out about Legion sexting with other women, we weren't even sleeping in the same bed anymore.

After our marriage imploded, the physical side of me took over with WM, despite the fact that I still felt lost emotionally. When I told him, "I don't want to feel anything," it was the realest yet saddest statement I think I had ever expressed. His response? "I got you." When I cried on his shoulder about Legion one night and said, "I don't know how this happened to me," WM did the best he could—bless his heart. He said, "Man, that nigga was on some bullshit." Hey, it wasn't getting any deeper than that. And honestly, these responses were fine for me at the time, because he was still giving me ten times more than what I'd gotten from my ex-husband.

Believing you're worthy is one thing, but acting on that belief is another. That's the piece that was missing with *anyone* I ever entertained who didn't deserve access to me but got it anyway. I didn't yet know what it looked like to love myself at full volume, so I chose what I was used to. But what we're used to isn't always what we deserve. Familiarity rarely means safety or love. Most of the time it just means you've learned to survive something that's breaking you.

I couldn't talk about what really weighed on my mind with WM. I couldn't be emotionally "naked" with him in any way. Physically?

Sure. But having deep conversations where I poured out my heart, my fears, my highs, and my lows? No, we didn't have that. I couldn't share how conflicted I was, because all I ever wanted was to be married and have a family, and yet here I was in a whirlwind of something entirely different. We had an understanding—nothing more, nothing less.

WM was even more of a comfort for me after what I went through with Beavis. There was a huge sense of relief and affirmation: I could once again tell myself that I wasn't hideous, because *this* man had no issue with my body and was willing to be seen with me if I allowed it. Whatever Beavis was talking about, whatever he thought, I felt affirmed by WM because there was someone who loved my curves. Then there was Legion, who gave me that plus what I thought was more.

Still, I knew there was a difference between a man who could blow your back out and one who could feed your soul—a huge difference. I was never going to have a home with WM, but I turned to him time after time to help me feel better. He was the subject of the "God, if he ain't for me, remove him" prayer I REFUSED to pray for a very long time. Sometimes it takes going through some real ugly bullshit to realize, *This isn't even what I want. This isn't helping me.* Yeah, WM gave me incredible orgasms, but I still felt empty when I got up. My level of self-worth was low. Too many times, after we were done spending time together, I would find myself just feeling numb. I knew I should feel like I was worth more than a casual fling, but honestly, I didn't believe it.

WM fulfilled a physical need in me, not an emotional one. But he didn't fulfill a mental need. What I really needed was a hug. I needed a shoulder I could cry on more than a dick to ride on. (My mother just read that and passed out. Sorry, Mom.) That whole "get over one guy by getting under another one" saying is cute and funny, but in the end, it prolongs everything that we are trying to do to heal. It delays those feelings of true worthiness and prevents us from propelling ourselves forward. Was there a part of me that found some element of my worth in the fact that WM always came back to me too? Perhaps. But that wasn't enough, and I'd started to feel it.

Some people might read this and say, "Oh, Reesa, you were just for the streets," but in my mind, it was different. Maybe I was naive, but I didn't think I was for the streets because my behavior was contained within my own little cocoon. WM was part of my circle. I didn't put myself out there for strangers or get intimately involved with every single man I met. When I say I tended to return to what I knew, to what was comfortable, that's exactly what I mean. I didn't spin the block with someone new, and that felt like I was not being promiscuous at all, actually. But it did mean that WM was a distraction. And I don't knock him for that—I gave him that role in my life. Emotional intimacy was never part of the terms and conditions of our arrangement, so it was up to me to finally decide it was a waste of my time and stop letting him soothe me every time I was in pain. I needed to allow myself to sit in the hurt for a bit and deal with my issues.

Only a few months prior to writing this, I finally decided to try something different. To stop running back to what's familiar. Because I realized that all it really does, in a way, is keep the cycle going. I had been putting myself right back into rotation, into a rut where, yes, someone fulfills my physical needs, but that's it—and it only delays me from doing the work I need to do on myself. And from meeting someone new. Now, for the first time, I'm intentionally sitting in the quiet. No distractions. No other opinions. There's just me asking myself, *What do I truly want? What do I deserve?*

It's easy for anyone to hear my story and say, "You didn't know your worth." They can chalk it up to some low self-esteem that exists without context. But the truth is, the reason some of us don't know our worth is that we never allow ourselves to be sad. I get really irritated when I hear someone telling people not to feel what they are feeling, because this is often the result. We never learn how to actually grieve a relationship's end, so we just bounce back and forth between the new and old. The distraction feels right.

When I think about those old patterns of mine, I don't feel shame anymore. What I feel is compassion for that version of me who was trying not to fall apart. She thought that staying with the mess she understood was somehow safer than stepping into the unknown. She was grasping at anything and anyone to avoid facing the void. I don't judge her, but I don't want to be her again. I no longer want to assign people roles that they were never qualified to play, and I don't want to go backward out of habit. And when the ache of loneliness shows up, I no longer want to confuse it with lack.

As I mentioned before, the loneliness is real. I know for a fact that even the judgy girls who read this and say, "I would never," experience those same feelings of loneliness in their quiet moments. The longing to just feel okay, to feel affirmed in their bodies. Those are things all of us want, regardless of where we are in life. There are people who have been married for almost twenty years who still want that same affirmation. But I'm grateful that I finally got to the point where I don't try to fill my void with old flames or false promises. I know I am enough and *worthy* of a love that honors both who I am and who I'm becoming.

It's way too easy to run back to what we've known, whether it is an old pattern or an old person. We believe that even if that situation hurt us, at least we knew how to manage that hurt. But healing? Aw, hell. *That's* unknown territory. And some of us are afraid of the unknown. The idea of uncertainty feels more terrifying than the pain we already understand.

Can I be honest? I'm not one of those women who will say, "Oh, I'm on a healing journey, so I've said no to all men." You can be on a healing journey and still want your head in the pillow sometimes. That's one of the things I wrestle with. I grew up in the church, and sometimes I filter my answers through the lens of *what will my mama think?* instead of being true to me.

But the real me will say, *Honey, if you need to get your back blown out while you're on a healing journey, then get your back blown out.* If you want to abstain or be celibate, that's fine too. It might even be good. For me, right now, the reason I'm not sleeping with WM is simple: I just don't feel like it. Yes, I want to be able to "go deep" with my partner and ultimately experience love again. But right now, I'm riding on the "I don't want to" train, and that works for me. I know there might come a time when I *will* feel like it. I will *want* to, and I don't want to pretend that I'm suddenly Gandhi and have taken on some holy stance that I haven't.

I am a very selective person, and maybe that's why I tend to go back to who I know and who I'm comfortable with, but I will say this: If you choose to return to that familiar place, at least be conscious as you do it. Know the risks. As your homegirl, I'm not going to judge you, as long as you're counting the cost and know what to expect (and what not to). Make your own choices, but recognize that you may feel, at the end of it, the same way you've always felt. That's the trade-off, right? You're trading that pleasure for the feeling that comes when he walks out the door.

And if you're okay with that, prepare for it. Ask yourself, *What can I do to take care of myself afterward?* Because you know those feelings are coming. Maybe you say, *I'm going to do this because my body needs it,* but when he leaves, you've already planned some kind of self-care. Maybe you'll take care of your heart by calling your homegirl, having a drink with her, and talking it out. Do whatever it takes. Because while you might've felt like you needed to do what you did in the moment, you know the emptiness that sometimes comes afterward needs tending.

When I started back up with WM after Legion, I did exactly this. I was very specific and intentional about what I wanted from him in our encounters, and I knew what I needed to do for myself after them. I was clear: "I don't feel like having a conversation. I don't care how your day was or how your week has been. I just want this to be about me. When we're done, you can get dressed and go." No, I wasn't letting him spend the night. No, we weren't going to lie there with Luther Vandross playing, all cuddled up. After he left, I thought about how I might tend to my heart. It was interesting, though, that when I finally created a boundary by saying no the last time we talked, it felt like I had moved to the next level of completely breaking the pattern.

To finally break those patterns, though, it's important to start with honesty. Be honest with yourself. Ask yourself, *Is this connection, no matter the shape or form, giving me peace, or is it just numbing my pain?* Not every good time is a healthy time. Some relationship dynamics are like sugar: They taste sweet in the moment, but they leave you sick in the end.

Even now, part of my journey toward embracing self-worth is managing my self-doubt. Throughout the process of writing this book, I've struggled with the voices in my head that try to tell me that I have no business telling my story in this form. That I am not worthy of any compassion for my journey, and that no one is going to read it anyway. In those moments, I have to remind myself that everyone may not love it. Yes, there will be people who won't appreciate my words. And yet I'm still worthy of writing them. Then I have to revel in those days when I am feeling myself—because I have them too. There are days when I say to myself, *Girl, you are Reesa Teesa. You were just a regular woman who told her story in her car, and somehow, 500 million views later, you have literally changed the game of storytelling online when it comes to social media. Nobody can ever take that away. There will be other Reesa Teesas, but you, bitch, are the first one.* Yep, part of building my self-worth is hyping myself up too.

So above all else, remember your worth, friend. And not in the clichéd way either. Your worth isn't something someone else assigns you. It's not based on how desirable or available or agreeable you are. Your worth, and my worth, exist because *we exist.* We don't have to perform or beg or break ourselves down to be loved, because the love that's meant for us will never require us to abandon ourselves.

Friends have asked me if I'm really done with WM. If I'm ready to move away from that toxic familiarity. I'm certainly trying. Life has a way of humbling you. You can travel here and there, do interviews, appear on *Good Morning America,* and still come home to an empty, quiet house. You can have the whole world know your name, and yet, no one knows the real you, the scared you, the shy you, the intimidated you, the you that feels all alone in a very crowded world. Those are the thoughts that echo inside me. Those are also the things I've realized I can't talk to WM about. I'm finally at a stage in my life where conversation—*real* conversation—matters deeply.

So let me tell you what I have done. I'm sure you know what

I'm going to say: I simply prayed. I said, "God, I know he's not supposed to be in my life. I do not have the willpower to walk away, so I'm asking that you peacefully remove him." What I meant by that—because I've learned to be specific with the Lord—was, "Don't kill him. Don't take him out of here. Don't hurt him. Just remove that portion of me that wants him."

But you know what? Even this idea of praying and asking God to take away the desire for someone because I didn't have the willpower to walk away is changing now. It feels like God is giving me my agency back. Not just by taking the desire away or removing the person from my life but by helping me *practice* advocating for what I really want for myself. As a result of *that* practice, and not necessarily some supernatural intervention outside of me, I've ended up not even having the taste for it anymore.

I think that's important, because sometimes those of us who grew up in the church will say things like, "Oh, I'm just going to pray. God's going to take it." But then we end up feeling some type of way when He doesn't remove that thing or person or feeling in the time frame we think He should. But all along, the lesson was for us to start advocating for ourselves—standing in the clarity we have been given and making a different choice. The removal of that person or thing from our lives becomes a result of our practice. And maybe as we practice saying no more, we'll get stronger, even to the extent that we no longer need God's intervention in those moments because we can intervene for ourselves. I believe God is proud of us when that happens.

Here's another truth bomb: I won't say yet that I'll never deal with WM again. *I know, I know.* I'm not there yet. I'm taking it one test at a time, because that's what it feels like: a test. Some people might say, "God doesn't test you like that," and maybe He doesn't.

But that's how it feels. Just before I went to France in mid-2025, WM reached out. "What you doing tonight?" he texted. I knew what that meant. My response? "I can't." He replied, "What do you mean *no*?" Normally, I didn't say no. In fact, there were times in the past when he said to me, "You know you can tell me no, right?" But I never did—until this moment. I texted back, "I can't. I'm getting ready to fly out in the morning. It's just not a good time." We went back and forth, and I eventually said, "Look . . ."—and I had to close my eyes when I hit send—"I'm not in the mood." Then I put my phone on Do Not Disturb, turned over, and went to sleep.

It may seem small, but doing that was a big deal for me. WM usually knows exactly what to say and do, and he runs the playbook well. But I finally asked myself, *Do you really feel like having him come over tonight?* And my honest answer was, *I don't.* I literally said to myself, *I don't feel like limping through the airport tomorrow.*

(I told you not to judge me.)

I'm learning to ask, in the privacy of my own thoughts, *Do you really feel like going through that? Do you really feel like answering this text? Do you really feel like picking up that phone call?* And if the answer is no, I give myself permission to follow through with the no. That whole conversation with WM was me testing that out, I think. And that was our last conversation. But if he reaches out again, I'll have to once again ask myself, *Do you feel like having a conversation?*

And you know what? I've found that my ability to do that with WM has translated into my being able to do that in other areas of my life. *Do you feel like talking to this person? Do you feel like answering this email, or do you just want to come back to it later?* That's what agency means for me. Agency feeds my feelings of self-worth. And this gives me permission to follow through on whatever my answer is. There's no one around to convict me. There's no one around to taint my thoughts. If it comes down to me saying, *I don't feel like it,* then I'm going to be okay with that. I'm allowed to want more. To stop settling. I'm allowed to say, "This isn't enough for me," and walk away without guilt.

Now I haven't blocked WM yet, so y'all continue to keep me in prayer, okay?

PART 2

What I Found

8

I Finally Started Listening to My Intuition

Listening to your inner voice is the ultimate act of self-love.

AS I'VE SAID PREVIOUSLY, my intuition had been screaming for a while that Legion wasn't doing right, but I never fully engaged that part of me besides simply recognizing that something didn't feel good about what he was doing and saying. Beyond that, I decided I would ignore what I was feeling—that is, until I couldn't anymore. Until I had to move past waiting for proof to come to me and go after the proof myself. Granted, I still felt like I needed some kind of proof. I wasn't willing to trust my gut alone, but I had moved on from my initial obliviousness by trying to actively uncover the lies. The question then became whether I would honor what I learned.

By May and June of 2021, after Legion and I had gotten married, after I found out that he'd been sexting other women, I had become an expert investigator. I was the FBI, the CIA, and the Department of Homeland Security all wrapped up in one determined Black girl body. No, really, I was obsessed with sniffing out his lies—and I did. And after I uncovered one lie, our whole life together became as shaky as a house of cards. One lie pulled loose, and suddenly everything started collapsing. I was talking to his ex-wife, looking up records, running background checks, and overall committed to figuring out who in the hell I had married. Sadly, in the midst of that, it never occurred to me to stop and open up to my family. I never even considered it. I couldn't deal with anyone else's reactions. I believed, rightly or wrongly, that judgment was waiting for me on the other side of those conversations, and my whole focus at this point was lining up the lies.

ONE OF THE EARLIEST LIES I uncovered took place when Legion sent me a photo of his company car, a BMW 5 Series sedan. It was charcoal gray, and it was parked in front of what he said was his building. I studied the picture closely. We had just finished another argument about why he couldn't bring the work car home. There was ALWAYS an excuse as to why we couldn't just drive up to Midtown and pick up this freakin' company car. So I stared at the picture on my phone. I slowly closed my eyes and let out a deep sigh. I sighed because I knew. My heart knew, my mind knew, and my spirit knew: He was lying.

Look up the photo, a voice inside said.

I took a deep breath and went to Google. I had no idea how to do a reverse Google image search, but I knew it existed. So I looked up the instructions and followed the steps. When I put in the photo Legion had sent me, sure enough, that image came up in the results. It was a photo that belonged to some random website. There was no way the photo he had sent me was actually his, and even though I already knew in my body that it wasn't, I had to see it. Once I saw it, I had to finally say out loud, "You married a liar." Now how deep did these lies go? This was the million-dollar question in my mind. I knew he told a lie here and there, but my mind couldn't fathom how diabolically deep the lies went.

He had sent me plenty of photos over the course of our relationship. Some were of his house in San Diego and his previous car, which had been conveniently "wrecked" just before he moved to Georgia. He'd also sent our realtor a photo of his bank statement with USAA, which was sent over to me. I did a reverse Google image search for each of these things, and every last one belonged to some unknown website. None of them belonged to Legion—not one single photo.

The more I looked up the photos, the more my hands were shaking. My brain was running at one hundred miles an hour. Questions were pouring out of my head. I didn't even know where to start. I sat in stunned silence, trying to slow my brain down so I could think. My intuition was quiet at this point. She had done all the yelling she could do. My heart was beating so hard in my chest that I was in actual physical pain as each search result appeared, exposing lie after lie.

"Breathe, Tareasa," I whispered to myself as I rubbed my chest and squeezed my eyes shut.

I must have sat there for fifteen minutes. Finally, I pulled up San Diego State University's website. I looked up the Office of the Registrar. I couldn't find any records of Legion ever being enrolled at San Diego State. Again, I knew, but I HAD to see it. With COVID restrictions slowly being lifted, there were some things I could verify and others I couldn't. But the damage was done.

I think the scariest part of all this was that my intuition never left me. She was with me the whole time. But she was also done with me. By the time I used reverse Google image searches to identify all those lies, I truly believe my intuition was on the couch with a blanket over her head, saying, "Bitch, I've been telling you this for months. I've used a bullhorn, flare guns, and pigeons. I've told you every way possible that something is wrong." But as I said in a previous chapter, she was just waiting for the other parts of me to get on the same page. That night, when I ran those reverse image searches, everything finally aligned. Every time I got that feeling in the pit of my stomach when Legion gave an excuse or changed the subject or deflected with a story about his being "a private citizen," things aligned further.

One of the more painful parts of coming into alignment with my intuition was revisiting every moment I had dismissed myself. There was the time Legion gave a shaky explanation about a supposed "business trip" and I told myself not to be insecure. There was the time he got cagey about his phone and I chalked it up to him "needing space." To this day, I struggle to trust that someone is actually speaking to another person when they answer the phone in my presence. This is all because I'd caught Legion numerous times talking to someone "from work"—only to learn later that the phone calls were never real. There were arguments about things that didn't even make sense that left me spinning. He made me feel like I was crazy for asking questions, and the truth is, that's a tactic. It's called gaslighting. And the danger of it is not just the lies someone else tells; it's the lies you start telling yourself. I confused suspicion with intuition. Suspicion is fear-based. Intuition is truth-based.

Thankfully, though, the spell was finally broken. I was done overriding the warning signals in my body in the name of love. I just needed to figure out how I was going to get out of it. I had to be strategic, because I knew Legion would go to any lengths to create doubt in me about what I wanted to do. There was so much noise in my head that I had to beg God to help me. Legion never gave me peace. He always had a story or an excuse about something, so that I couldn't keep any of it straight and felt like I was going crazy. I wasn't sleeping well, and I had to take sleeping pills to knock me out. When he was awake, he never stopped talking, so I had to steal moments of peace and solitude. When I say I had to be strategic, I mean I had to play chess while he was playing checkers.

Legion's lies were like a loose thread on an old sweater. If you pull one, you will inevitably end up unraveling everything. In fact, there were so many things he lied about that, ultimately, he moved out of our primary bedroom because of one of them—a lie about a condition that had begun to interrupt our intimacy. But God is not only funny sometimes, He's strategic. I now know that Legion moving out of the primary bedroom was the start of God helping me to get out of the relationship. It was like He was saying, "I'm getting ready to orchestrate a series of things that will give you clarity. Number one: He is going to move into another room. The reason he's moving into that other room doesn't have anything to do with his health. It is because you need to hear Me more than you hear him." Up until that point, I rarely had time to just be quiet and think, because Legion talked constantly from the time he woke up to the time he went to bed. It was almost like he was talking so much and so fast so that I couldn't remember what he was saying. He overwhelmed me with information, which is why I doubted myself.

So Legion moving into the guest room was an opportunity for some peace and quiet. I could go over in my mind what I felt and knew. I could unpack what I could and could not prove. If I'm being honest, I still struggled, even after making my decision and planning my escape. I'd been taught my whole life that God hates divorce. But there came a point when I remember saying, "I'm just going to need His forgiveness, because I can't stay in this." No, I did not file for divorce because of what was going on with him physically. That was simply God saying, "I need to move him out of this room so I can get her alone. I'm going to make it so the very thing that she once loved cuddling up next to is no longer available."

On June 17, I finally saw the conditions he was living under in that room when I walked in. There were Powerade bottles and clothes everywhere. And the smell? Oh, my goodness, it was horrible. I realized in that moment that I hadn't been paying attention at all to what was going on in my own home. I had been consumed with finding out what Legion had been lying about. I would come home, eat alone, clean the kitchen, say hello, and go into my bedroom to start investigating. This was the first time I had stopped and really looked at my husband. It looked like he'd lost a lot of weight in a short span of time. It was so bad that the "C" word crossed my mind.

What I saw served as a catalyst. I walked into the room with no intention of discussing all the evidence of his lies I had found over the previous few weeks. My desire was to simply have a conversation about us breaking up. I was calm, cool, and collected, because I was just planning to lay out how I was feeling. But I guess my heart wanted one more shot at bat. I asked him one last time.

"We need to talk," I said. I sat on the end of the bed, facing the window. I brought my knee up to my chin, a sign that I wasn't trying to fight but just to have a conversation.

"Did you really go to San Diego State?" I asked softly.

He sighed, annoyed at my question.

"Yes, we have been over this so many times," he whined.

"Then why don't they have any record of you being a student?" I asked. I was still calm.

"Because I was a private citizen."

I knew he was going to say that. I just had to hear it one last time.

I closed my eyes and shook my head. "I bet you've never even been to California. I bet you've never even been outside the East Coast."

All my emotions came to the surface, but I remained calm at first.

"I'm willing to bet that Georgia, Pennsylvania, and Rhode Island are the only places you've been." There was silence on his end, and it was loud. Finally I told him the pure truth.

"I don't want this anymore."

"What? Our marriage?" he asked.

"I don't want you anymore. I don't want this—I don't want this marriage." I said it as calmly as I could.

"That's not how marriage works," he tried to protest.

I shook my head. I was so done.

That's when he got on the phone and called a family member. "My wife don't want me anymore. She said I've been lying to her. I ain't never lied to her."

That's when all hell broke loose.

I could have broken down all the evidence of his lies. I could have mentioned the second ex-wife I'd found (he had already denied the first one). But I did not want to tell him what I'd found, because I needed to be very sure that, no matter what he said, I was still leaving. I knew he would've had a response for everything. I was finally clear about who I was dealing with, and I would not be swayed.

In hindsight, I realize that when I went into that room, it was almost like I was not truly there. I wasn't trying to go off. My intuition had gotten off the couch and said what she said. It was my heart that needed the confirmation. I mostly wanted us to come to an agreement that this was not going to work—to be adults about it. I certainly was not expecting it to go the way it went.

Just because I was able to finally break away from Legion didn't mean the pain disappeared overnight. Nor did it eliminate the long-term trauma caused by my refusal to stop resisting what I knew. I had to understand that I didn't need all the proof to take a step in the direction of truth. I didn't have to wait for the house to burn down before I could acknowledge that I smelled smoke. I could trust the smoke. I could trust the temperature shift. I could trust myself.

As I've said, that's hard for me, even now. I often wish there was a way to know without a doubt that someone won't hurt me—that way I wouldn't have to rely so much on my ability to trust my gut. Unfortunately, that's not how it works.

I know there may be somebody who's reading this and saying, "I definitely don't want to go through what you went through, but I still want to try to have my turn." I get that. You want to trust yourself enough to be able to engage in the serious talk of a relationship, but you also want to know that you'd be willing to walk away if something doesn't look right.

Well, for me, it's taken practice. What I mean by that is that I'm learning to practice trusting myself and trusting my intuition outside of any romantic entanglements, so that by the time I find myself in one, it will very much be a part of how I already move.

I'm thankful that my relationship with my intuition isn't completely broken, but I clearly don't have a strong history of listening to it. I've spent years arguing myself out of what I felt or sensed, always asking, *What if I'm wrong?* Now I wrestle with a different question: *Is this truly my intuition, or am I planting seeds because of what I've been through?* Trauma has a way of blurring things. So these days, I slow down and ask myself more intentionally: *What is my gut actually saying? What am I discerning here?* That's in pretty much every area of my life. I observe more. I watch. I pause.

For example, there's a woman I know. She's older than me, a Black woman, and at first glance, she seemed like a potential friend. But there are things about her personality that feel familiar to me in a way I don't like. I've said to my best friend, "I feel like I've seen this movie before."

I wouldn't call her a mean girl, but she's very aggressive. She cuts people off quickly. And while I fully believe in boundaries—if someone does you dirty, you don't owe them access—I also believe in grace. She doesn't leave room for that. Her energy gives off subtle frenemy vibes.

The old version of me would lean in anyway. I would have told myself that I need to "accept people as they are." And I suppose there's some truth in that. But this newer version of me says, "Don't do too much yet. Observe." And that's what I'm doing. I'm humble enough to admit that my discernment isn't perfect, but something in me says that if I ever do or say something this woman doesn't like, she'll cut me off without hesitation. I've known women like this before—women who move through life with a cutthroat mentality.

Of course, I don't know what made her that way. Maybe she's been hurt, or maybe she's been betrayed one too many times herself. I don't know. But because I recognize that energy, I don't treat her like a close friend. I don't confide in her. Anything I share with her is information she could find on Google. My gut tells me that she's someone who feels the need to compete with certain women for attention, sometimes even for men. And I don't compete. I don't have the energy for it. I don't want to. If there's a competition, you win. Congratulations! I'll hand you the crown myself. I still haven't fully put my finger on what's up with this woman yet, but I'm proud of myself for being willing to listen to what the Spirit is telling me *and* acting on it.

That's the thing with intuition: Its presence is felt, but so is its absence. I've known my good friend Shawn since 2014. We both worked together at Georgia State Patrol. We have been through a lot together. I've been there for her, and she has been there for me through thick and thin. This woman took me to the hospital when I had to have my D&C. She is a friend. If Shawn tells me something, I give her the benefit of the doubt. I believe her.

My intuition has not ever yelled at me about Shawn. It's quiet. I've been in her mama's house. I've been in her sister's house. If she shows me something, I believe it. If she tells me something, I believe it. We have a relationship. History. An understanding. That understanding has taught me that I can also use the absence of conflict, the absence of my intuition's warnings, as a gauge when dealing with people. Is my intuition active? Are the questions and concerns firing off? Or is there peace?

That same intuition shows up in other areas too—especially in platonic relationships with men. There's a guy I've gone to lunch with occasionally. It's a total friend zone. He's been featured on my Instagram, and we would grab lunch once a month—nothing romantic. Recently he told me he'd been seeing someone and that it was becoming somewhat serious. Once I understood that, I chose to fall back. If he called and wanted to talk, I'd listen. But I stopped initiating lunch meetups.

Why, Reesa? If you all are friends, why did you stop?

Part of that decision had more to do with *her* than with him. As

I asked him follow-up questions, it became clear that things felt more serious on her end than he was letting on. She was offering him space in her life. I've been that woman before. I know what that place feels like.

Meanwhile, he kept saying, "I'm single until I get married." I didn't want any part of that. I know what it's like to care deeply while the other person keeps their options emotionally open. So I asked myself again, *What is your intuition telling you?* And the answer was clear: *Leave him alone.*

If this man ever asks why we stopped going out to lunch, I have no problem telling him the truth: *I didn't know you were involved with someone. Now that I do, I'm respectfully stepping back. I want you to be happy. I want you to do right by her, but I'm not going to be part of this dynamic.*

The last time we had lunch, he talked a lot—more than he probably realized. He said it wasn't serious, but he had multiple photos of her. He said he wasn't in love, though he "loved her." He joked that if she played her cards right, she could be the next ex–Mrs. Last Name. They'd talked about marriage. The whole time, she was texting him repeatedly, asking where he was, when he was coming home, whether he was still out with me.

He told me she was fine with us hanging out. And for the record, *I* wasn't worried. We were just friends. But my gut spoke clearly at that table: "This is the last time y'all are doing this, and he doesn't even know it yet."

When I told Shawn later, she asked if I was catching feelings. I wasn't. I just didn't want to be part of a situation where a man says he's single while a woman clearly has real feelings invested in him. I've been her. I won't assist in hurting someone else that way, even unknowingly.

What my intuition told me loud and clear was that he was trying to paint a picture that wasn't fully accurate. And I chose to honor that gut feeling by stepping away. No drama or jealousy. No competition. Just clarity.

This is where I am now when it comes to my intuition and discernment. In some situations, I make a clear decision and exit. In others, I observe, try to recognize the patterns, and try to act on what I'm seeing. Sometimes I get it wrong, but I'm getting better.

I recently went to Mexico for a solo trip. And it was horrible. It was pure shenanigans at every turn. I made a video for social media about how bad it was, and there's a reason. I'm so sick and tired of seeing people only posting about their perfect trips. If you had a great trip, that's wonderful, but can we just keep it a little real? Sometimes the trip does not go the way you thought it was going to go. For me, it was probably not the best use of wisdom to take the trip in the first place, because there was something in me that said, *I don't think you should go to Mexico. I don't think this is the time to have a solo trip.* Being me, I went back and forth with myself. I had booked the tickets and found the resort. I just wanted to go somewhere—to see the water, lie on a couch, and read a book or listen to music. Just vibe out.

In my head, I knew exactly what I was trying to do, but the trip went nothing like that. My intuition, in many ways, was trying to tell me that the trip I wanted and the trip I'd booked were very different. She nudged me to do more digging to see if I would even enjoy the trip. But I didn't do that. I wanted to treat myself, by any means necessary.

I made that video trying to acknowledge that, hey, sometimes we have good intentions and the execution just isn't right. Sometimes there is something in us that says, *Maybe you should postpone that for another time. Maybe you should do a little bit more research.* I didn't, and—well, lesson learned. This wasn't as big of a lesson as "Who TF Did I Marry?" but it was a lesson that hit the pockets, because I paid money to go somewhere and did not enjoy it at all. I left more exhausted than when I came. That is the by-product of me not listening to myself. I should've just canceled the plane ticket, got myself a voucher, canceled the resort reservation, and gone another time. But no—instead I dealt with iguanas all around the place, mosquito bites up and down my back, a peacock on-site that sang all night long. So even now, I still have moments when I don't listen. It's just that the cost is different. There's a consequence for not listening to your intuition, and an even greater one for not honoring it.

Listening would have meant saying, *Maybe I shouldn't take this trip.* Acting would have meant saying, *Let me just do a little research. Oh, they got iguanas and a peacock? No, thank you.* Honoring my intuition would have meant saying, *Let me cancel this ticket and think of something else to do.*

Your intuition will be screaming at you in ways that you will actually hear sometimes. That's always been my belief. And I do believe that every person's intuition is unique to them—meaning your intuition knows how to let you know. It's not going to sound the same as mine. I've always believed that your intuition is a gift from the Holy Spirit. If that is the case, then the Holy Spirit knows how to talk to you so that you actually hear Him. How He talks to you is not how He talks to me. How He talks to me is not how He talks to the next person. It could be something very simple, but it's impactful to you.

I used to think that embracing intuition was only for "deep" people—you know, the ones who sage their homes and do meditation retreats and read energy. But no. It's not about rituals or religion; it's about your relationship to your own spirit. Embracing my intuition didn't save me from the heartbreak, but it saved me from staying stuck. It gave me a way to return to myself. The road to healing started the moment I stopped fighting the truth. The moment I stopped asking for more evidence. The moment I looked at my own reflection and said, "I believe you."

9

I Reclaimed My Power

Take back your power, one choice at a time.

ALL HELL BROKE LOOSE IN MY HOUSE after I confronted Legion about ending our marriage. There was lots of screaming and yelling and name-calling. But let me tell you something I've never said before: It scared me how angry I got that day. I remember, with a terrifying kind of clarity, making peace with the fact that, if he had said or done the wrong thing, I might have been going to jail that day.

Some of my anger was pure hurt. It was that kind of unfiltered rage that grips your whole chest. All I knew was that this creature (because that's how I saw him at that point) had to get the hell out of my house. I know now that some of my anger was misplaced. If he'd told his family member a month earlier, "My wife thinks I lied to her. I ain't never lied to her," it probably wouldn't have sent me into a rage the way it did that day. So much of my vitriol was rightly directed at him, but in some ways, much of it was also aimed at myself. I was so mad at myself because I could not believe I ended up with someone who had lied to this degree.

It was almost unfathomable. I kept thinking about all the things that didn't make sense, but to go so far as to say, *I think I married a pathological liar*? It was still hard to grasp. The day it all came to a head, I know that anger wasn't just about him. It was also about me. *Ain't no way on God's green earth this should be happening to me.*

However, it wasn't just that I was mad at him or at myself. It was also months of buildup that finally erupted. I'd finally tuned in to my spirit, and nothing was panning out. Every promise Legion made fell apart. So it wasn't as if I woke up angry on June 17. I'd been angry for a while, but I had pushed it down, again and again. So as things made less and less sense, I got angrier. I'm one of those people who gets upset when things don't add up. I don't like confusion or chaos. They frustrate me. And honestly, I don't handle that frustration well. I tend to get emotional. So from January to June, it was frustration on top of frustration that finally came to an emotional head.

After all the screaming and yelling, Legion finally left the home we shared. He got in his car and drove off. I watched him turn the corner and disappear out of the subdivision where we lived. The moment he was gone, I locked the door behind him. Then I sat on the stairs. I hadn't really cried yet, and I wouldn't for a while. I just sat there.

In a way, I am grateful for the anger I was feeling when I let him go. It was a kind of protection in that moment. When I'm angry, it propels me to act. It's like, *No, the hell you didn't.* Afterward, I might grieve, but in that moment, the anger kept me moving toward closure. If I had been more sorrowful instead of angry, he might've talked me down. The anger kept me focused enough to get him out of the house rather than falling into that whole pitiful, *Why did you do this to me?* which would've been another opening for his manipulation. My anger also meant that I didn't have the space to second-guess myself like I had before.

Think, Tareasa. Breathe, Tareasa. Think, Tareasa.

Sitting on those stairs, I repeated those words over and over again like a chant. Like they were holy. The more I said them, the calmer I got. And then, clear as day, I heard the question, "What do you want to do?"

Six words. That's all it took. That one question cracked open the door that had been bolted shut in my chest. It gave me back the pen to write my own script and the permission to act on my own behalf. That question became a mantra that still lives with me. I whisper it in the shower. I say it out loud in the car. It comforted me on June 17, 2021, and it still comforts me today.

But back then, the question led me to create a road map. I needed something linear that my brain could latch on to that would allow me to feel safe and in control again.

Change the security codes.

Go to Home Depot and get new locks (with the landlord's permission).

Get somebody to install them.

Buy trash bags and storage totes.

Purge.

Clean.

File for divorce.

That was the list. Now it was time to get to work.

After securing the home, my first task was to clean. I needed to put my space back together again after what had just happened. I walked into the bathroom, and that's when I found it: Legion had taken a shit in the bathtub.

No, you didn't read that wrong. *In. The. Bathtub.* Like a calling card. Like a middle finger on the way out. In that moment, the symbolism hit me like a freight train. This man had taken a shit on my life. He had wrecked it completely. That bathtub became a metaphor, and once I saw it that way, I knew I had a choice. I could stay stuck in disgust and rage, or I could grab the bleach, run the shower to rinse that mess, and drain his shit out of my life.

So that's what I did.

(And when I left that bathroom, I called a professional cleaner to do the rest.)

When I confronted Legion about it on the phone, he claimed that he wasn't able to make it to the toilet. Yet the toilet is closer to the door than the bathtub—so once again, his lies made no damn sense.

RECLAIMING MY POWER didn't happen all at once. It didn't come in a lightning bolt of revelation. It was more of a slow fire. I didn't have time in the beginning to process what had happened either. I only had enough bandwidth to do the next right thing for me.

Legion left June 17, 2021. I filed for divorce on my own by June 24. I used an online service and filled everything out, printed the paperwork, got it notarized, and sent it to the court—all within a week. When he'd left my house, I'd told Legion, "I don't give a fuck where you go." The family member who he had called that day said, "I'll send you money, just leave." Of course, I screamed, "Oh no! Why would you do that? He's got alllll this money, right? *Right?*"

Legion returned to his family in Philadelphia, and when he got there, he told his family that I had kicked him out. He also said I'd had an affair with someone at my job, and that the man had used his gun to threaten him. He even told multiple family members that *I'd* threatened him, and he tried to get my agency to start an internal investigation of me.

As the days passed, however, Legion's family and the people who'd known him for a long time didn't believe him. In fact, they confirmed what I already knew. One person even said, "He's always been a liar. The lies just got bigger as he got older."

On June 28, I started a new job. Yes, my marriage had ended spectacularly, *and* I was starting a new position at the same time. Every emotion was heightened, but I couldn't process it all. My mind was just in survival mode: *He's out. It is what it is. You've got to get your head together for this new job, Tareasa.* I was moving through my days on pure adrenaline. But eventually, reality would catch up to me.

By the second or third week at my new job, it hit me: Nothing I'd experienced with Legion was real. The waves of grief and emotion hit my heart. I had been obsessed with his lies for months. I was waking up every day, running background checks, checking Facebook, and getting calls from strangers. Even after our breakup, I was dealing with Legion's incessant calls and messages: "Why you got to be like this? We're married. It's not what you think." The chaos had officially exhausted me.

By August, I stopped it all. I'd had enough. Everything felt like a lie, so I wasn't taking any more calls from family or doing any more research. I didn't want to know anything else. It was finally time to start processing my feelings around what happened. It was time to reclaim my power. I wasn't going to ask myself anymore if Legion loved me, because I knew the answer. Honestly, I don't even think he liked me, based on how he played in my face. This was the most depressing time of my life. I was finally sitting with all my feelings, and it was painful . . . and ugly.

Once I moved at the end of August, I finally felt a sense of relief. I know it's cliché, but I was able to exhale for the first time. The divorce had cost money, but I'd saved enough to start over. I packed Legion's things with surgical precision and bagged up every remnant of that false life we had been living. Some might think I went to the extreme. If he'd touched it, it was gone—clothes, furniture, everything. I planned to enter that new home with nothing but my own clothes, and if he'd bought them, they weren't coming with me either. I sent him a written notice, which he acknowledged, giving him sixty days to come get everything or I would dump or donate it.

I ended up donating it all.

Slowly, once I moved in, I replaced every dish towel and every piece of furniture. That new home became a place to just *be.* It was my ICU, where I healed but wasn't yet whole. In some ways, it felt like rehab—a space for quiet reflection and recovery. I wasn't happy yet, but I wasn't who I was in the home with him either. My new space was where I could finally breathe. I could cry if I needed to. Years earlier, I'd grieved the end of my relationship with Beavis by playing Adele on repeat. In this home, even though I wasn't there very long, I listened to Beyoncé's *Renaissance* and found my dance again.

I wouldn't say that what I experienced in that transitional time was a false peace, but it was a peace mixed with deep sadness. You see, the quiet can be heavy too. I laughed all day with my new co-workers, but then I came home to silence. I knew why I couldn't shake off those feelings of being lost completely. I was still holding on to something. There was one final thing I hadn't let go of.

I still had Legion's last name.

When I think about why I kept his last name for so long, I imagine those priests from centuries ago who flogged themselves in repentance. Self-flagellation—that's exactly what it was. I punished myself for marrying Legion. To me, that name felt like a scarlet letter. I kept it as a reminder: *You made this bed, now lie in it.* It wasn't necessarily about trying to keep something from the marriage. Remember, I wanted nothing! It was more about the guilt and shame I carried.

On New Year's Eve 2023, nearly three years after our marriage ended, something finally clicked. I woke up and said, *It's time.* I didn't care how much it cost; I was going to do it. I was ready to change my name back. My friend Hannah, an attorney, told me, "Check your divorce decree first! It's probably already in there." And sure enough, it was. Once I changed my name back to Johnson in January, I changed my username on TikTok too. On social media, I became Reesa Teesa. Not long after, on February 14, the first episode of "Who TF Did I Marry?" went live. It was a short window but a powerful one. In fact, I get teary-eyed thinking about it because it felt like a symbolic shift—like the final tie being broken. It also ushered in what I now see as a form of restoration. I started getting back everything that had been stolen from me in my relationship with Legion. For me, reclaiming my power began with reclaiming my name. Of course, I didn't see it that way at the time. I just saw it as a form of acceptance, and a symbol of forgiving myself for all the mistakes I'd made. But as I began to pray more and listen to the Holy Spirit, not about a man or a relationship but about what God wanted for me next, I realized that there *was* a deliverance that needed to happen by returning to my maiden name: a release of everything that kept me bound to the past. This included Legion's last name. I don't think there would've been as much success if I'd still had that old name attached to my story. The internet would've twisted it, for sure, and said I kept the name for attention. It would have changed everything God was trying to do in my life going forward. It would have kept me on a plateau when God was very much about to take me higher.

I didn't realize until I started writing this book just how much things changed for me the moment I released his name. I thought it would cost me hundreds of dollars and months of my life to do it when, in fact, it took only eight minutes. I went to the Social Security office with my divorce decree, and eight minutes later the young woman I sat down with said, "Okay, you're all set." It's funny that eight is often viewed as a number that represents new beginnings. I guess even God has a sense of humor sometimes.

There are layers to reclaiming your power, but reclaiming your name is a huge one. I recently went so far as to trademark my brand name, Reesa Teesa. I didn't want anyone else to take it, because it now means something deeply personal to me. It represents what it took to get here. To some people, that might seem small. But behind closed doors, it's so much bigger. I'd held on to Legion's name out of shame. I battled all kinds of mental warfare around it. But I released it with a kind of courage and pride that had escaped me for most of my life. It was a reminder that I'd reached the point where I could say, *I don't want to be this person anymore.* Where I could choose to no longer be held back by my regrets.

I recently rewatched portions of my TikTok series, and I'm so grateful I was on a nighttime flight when I did, because I was crying as I watched it. Watching it made me recall exactly how everything felt in real time. With all the blessings and opportunities I have now, it's easy to forget how it *felt* in that moment. I sat on that plane wiping my tears not because I'd forgotten but because life has a way of moving on, and when you look back, it's incredible to see how far you've come. It also wasn't that I felt dumb all over again. It was more that I felt deep grief for the woman who'd gone through that—the woman who betrayed herself. For a moment, the *should*s washed over me: *I should've done this. I should've done that.* But there was also a tremendous amount of gratitude. People can call me desperate or dumb if they must. They can make whatever assumptions they want. Some people don't see the traumatic nature of the series, but others do. I've seen the shift in the comments around parts 37 or 38, where people started saying, "Yo, this isn't funny anymore." And they were right. It wasn't. But I'm still thankful I've finally reclaimed what's true: Legion may not have loved me, but I was (and still am) wholly and completely lovable. That's what watching it now reveals to me. Reclaiming my power gave me clarity and a love for myself that isn't up for debate anymore.

We don't always reclaim our power in loud ways. You may not post all your business on TikTok or make some big announcement. That's fine. Our power is often taken back in smaller, quieter decisions. The whispered "no." The phone call you don't return. The changed lock. The lawyer's retainer you pay. The therapy appointment you finally make. Every single one of those steps is galvanizing the universe to continue working on your behalf. It's setting your trajectory toward healing. You don't return the call *so* that you don't get sucked into another lie or more drama, *so* that you don't get that headache, *and* you sleep well, *and* you wake up rested and ready to tackle your purpose. Everything is connected. To be clear, this doesn't mean I never felt scared again. It certainly doesn't mean I didn't cry or rage or question myself from time to time. It does mean I made a choice to keep choosing me.

I must admit that reclaiming my power has not looked exactly the way I thought it would. Sometimes we imagine ourselves as some kind of Black girl ninja snatching back everything that was stolen from us with style and passion and panache. To the sisters who do exactly that, you have my deep admiration. But my reclamation has been slower. If I'm honest, I haven't fully gotten *me* back—not yet. I'm in the process of it, but it's unfinished. I'm still learning how to return to myself.

The power I *have* gotten back is the ability to embrace my peace. In fact, now that I'm writing my story, I'm wondering if *reclaiming* is even the right word, because I don't remember ever having this peace that I have now before. Maybe when I was a little girl, before I knew how hard life can be? But this peace I've claimed for myself now is simple and new. And compared to the past, it looks like simply knowing what I am and am not coming home to. That knowledge brings mental, emotional, and even physical relief.

My world—hell, my mind—feels different. I was shattered before. And I don't use that word lightly. *Shattered* means tiny pieces. There are things in my life and parts of me that will likely never go back to what they were. Because of that, I can't move through this season of my life thinking in terms of what has been *lost* or *regained*. Reclaiming power requires a kind of surrender to the newness of it all. I've said it a myriad of times throughout this book: I'm not healed or settled yet. I'm adjusting. Adjusting to a new normal. Adjusting to giving myself permission, one moment at a time.

I used to think that walking away from someone meant I had lost. That choosing myself meant I'd be alone. But choosing myself didn't isolate me; it anchored me. So if you feel like you've lost your power, let me remind you that it's not really gone. It might just be buried under the rubble of what has fallen apart in your life. The beautiful thing is that you can still dig it, and yourself, out. Power isn't something someone else gives you. It's something you realize you've had all along. Sure, the journey back to it might feel like a crawl, but it's still yours. Every choice you make in the direction of truth is a choice to stand in your power.

Nobody can define your healing but you. Nobody can write your comeback but you. Get rid of all that shame and guilt. It can't serve you right now anyway. You might just find yourself sitting on your own stairs, breathing your own name, and asking those questions that are now my favorite questions to ask: *What do you want to do? Who do you want to be? What's the next right thing?*

And then you do it.

Before you know it, you'll look up and realize you've built a life that honors who you are—one that reflects the strength it took to start over. And baby, let me tell you: When you truly remember who the hell you are, there is nothing and nobody that can stop you.

10

I Prioritized My Peace

Peace isn't a luxury;
it's a necessity for building a life.

THE MOMENT I WALKED INTO that new townhome, a rental in Cobb County, Georgia, after leaving Legion, I almost cried. There was a sense of physical peace that came with my new set of keys and change of address. We all deserve to breathe fresh air when we walk into our homes. I was so determined to have peace in my life that, to this day, I am very cognizant of who I allow to visit my home. I can count on one hand the number of people who have been in my home, because it's important to be around those who care about me and show that care in healthy ways—not because I am antisocial but because I now understand the true value of peace.

Unfortunately, I was only able to live in that house for a year because the landlord decided he wanted to sell it. This really upset me because I felt so good staying there. I was close to work and not far from family. For all intents and purposes, it was a really good deal for me. So, when I learned he was selling, I had only two months left on my lease and I had to scramble. Whatever peace I had gained was lost, because I had to allow strangers into my space to see it for showings. My stress level was through the roof, so once again I began looking for another place to live. It was so hard. The market was crazy. I was looking everywhere in Metro Atlanta, and every place I was interested in was either too expensive or had a move-in date that was too far out.

Thankfully, I eventually found a house in Jonesboro: a cute little white single-family home with three bedrooms and two baths. I signed a two-year lease because I did not want to find myself in a position where I would have to move again in one year. The downside was the house was an hour and a half away from work and an hour from family.

But God always has a plan, right? My long, lonely commute to work is what led me to join TikTok. I would show my commute to my followers while playing music. The camera was turned toward my windshield, so they were never looking at me. It was cathartic. Some days I'd play worship music, other days Cardi B.

When I first moved, my mom moved in with me. I love my mom. Oh, I do, I do, I do. She did the best she could at being a single mom and raising me. But after Legion, I just really wanted to heal, grieve, be angry, and be depressed—in private, with no one around. In truth, this was a difficult time in my relationship with my mom. I don't think she understood the emotionally dark and depressed place I was in. I was angry and mean, sometimes even disrespectful. I felt like I was in a walking hell because, in addition to my grief, I was dealing with bullshit at my job and a long, stressful commute—just to have to come home and wear a mask there too. I didn't feel like I could display the level of depression I was fighting because I didn't want my mom to preach to me about God's love and mercy. I didn't want to hear it. I just wanted to hide and be left alone.

Things shifted though when "Who TF Did I Marry?" blew up in 2024. Money and opportunities followed, and I was able to move my mom into her own place. This helped me find peace in my home again for a time. But after the story went viral, I was traveling a lot, and I was taking Ubers from my house to the airport. Uber drivers, regardless of their nationality or ethnicity, started to recognize me. "Oh, this is where you live? Oh my God, I know where Reesa Teesa lives." It became a safety concern. Home no longer felt like my sanctuary. When the whole world is talking about you, it doesn't take much for someone to do a quick search and find your address. Cars started driving slowly in front of my house. If you typed my name in Google, my address would come up. Once again, my peace was gone, but I wasn't necessarily worried about anything nefarious. I just knew in my spirit that it was time to go. There was a deep, undeniable urge to leave that space behind. It was time to shift again.

I'd started paying down my debts after the series went viral, and I finally had space to sit with myself and ask, *What do you actually want?* If I'm being honest, my first thought was the seventy-thousand-dollar car I'd always wanted. Before everything blew up, my goal in getting a better-paying job was simple: I wanted to be able to afford a dark blue BMW X5 with a cognac interior.

IN "WHO TF DID I MARRY?" I talked about a particular car I wanted. My ultimate dream car before I saw this one had been a Range Rover, but this ride was everything. With Legion, I had test-driven ten or fifteen different vehicles. While doing this I fell in love with a dark blue BMW X5 with black wheels and a cognac interior. I know—very specific. It was truly everything to me. Sure, it was the ultimate status symbol, but I also just felt good in it. Of course, as he usually did, Legion talked that talk. "This is the car I want for you. The one our kids will be safe in." And of course, I believed him until I didn't. We never purchased it, but it still stuck with me. It would always be one of my faves.

When the series went viral, people homed in on two things. The first was me wanting to go to London and Paris. The second was that BMW. I had mentioned other cars throughout the course of the series, but apparently the BMW stuck with those watching. The comments went crazy. Folks were tagging BMW. Other companies I mentioned started reaching out. It was a whirlwind for real. And there I was, just a regular chick in Georgia, reading the comments, thinking, *Oh my God*. Sure, it crossed my mind that BMW might see all the comments, but I wasn't thinking ten steps ahead.

Finally they did. Whoever was running BMW's social media accounts commented and said, "Everyone hold on, we're just catching up."

That's when things escalated. Not only did BMW enter the chat, another creator made a video telling BMW they needed to make sure Reesa Teesa got her BMW. A dealership in South Georgia even said they were "on their way" to help Reesa get her BMW. Finally BMW USA, the parent company, hits me in my DMs asking how they could get in contact with me. They said they wanted to talk to me about getting the X5.

See, BMW was getting a lot of publicity from my videos. There were people saying, "I just got Reesa's BMW," meaning a vehicle with the customizations I mentioned. So the way I interpreted the DMs and the emails between me, BMW, and my attorney, Olivia Harris, was that BMW was saying they would like to give me the use of the X5 for free. Was there a part of me deep down that questioned that? Yep. My intuition was whispering to proceed slowly and carefully.

But I was brand-new to this viral world. Of course, I know now that saying "We would like to get you the X5" and "We would like to give you the X5" are two totally different things. One word change—big difference. But back then, I wasn't as savvy or as knowledgeable about these things. So when Olivia got involved and started asking about terms, we ultimately learned that my assumptions were wrong, and the engagement fizzled out. It became apparent that one of two things had happened. Either the person we were emailing with didn't have the authorization to offer what he had offered, or I had misunderstood "We want to get you the X5."

Okay, fine. It is what it is, I thought. After some counsel, I chose not to make a video about the whole ordeal. No matter how I felt, I wasn't interested in siccing the entire internet on BMW because of a misunderstanding. I just moved on, because if there was one thing I was paying attention to, it was all the lessons I was learning in real time. My baptism into going viral felt more like drinking from a fire hydrant.

I let people online assume different things about the situation. Some folks said, "Oh, she doesn't have the money for it." Others were saying BMW had fumbled because this was a perfect opportunity for them to capitalize on the publicity and advertising my videos gave them and give me an X5 that they could later write off. And because the internet is predictable, there were still others who said, "She doesn't deserve a car. What makes her think she should get a car just because she told a story?"

I eventually made a TikTok about it and casually said, "This is the closest I'm going to get to an X5." It wasn't even a dig at BMW. It was just a nod to what had happened that nobody really knew about anyway because I had never "exposed any emails or DMs." But based on my comment, Hyundai actually responded: "We don't have an X5, but we think you'd look good in a blue Palisade."

Wait, what?!

So there we were again: me and Olivia, in conversation with Hyundai. The contact said, "We can get you a dark blue Palisade," but this time we were ready. We needed clarity on what he meant. Olivia asked what the terms were, and let's just say, Hyundai was not playing. Their contact said, "Oh, now. We'll give it to you for free and take care of everything. We'll do a one-year term, and then after that we'll renew and see where we're at. The car will be delivered to you."

I had the option of choosing the dark blue or the dark maroon SUV, and of course I chose the former. But it was going to take some time because it was in their shipping port in Savannah and had to be brought up to Metro Atlanta, where I lived. Nevertheless, Hyundai sent the contract, Olivia looked it over, and I signed it.

I had a car already: a little hatchback Mazda CX-3. Once I got the contract from Hyundai, I paid off the car I had and then drove to my aunt's house to give it to my little cousin. That's where they were going to deliver the Palisade. To be honest, until I drove to my aunt's house, a part of me was still unsure. It was like my intuition this time was trying to tell me that everything was okay—that this was a good thing happening and I should embrace it. But I was struggling to even hear that. I didn't settle into accepting what was happening until the driver texted saying he was about twenty minutes away. Then he showed up with a brand-new, dark blue Palisade with a white interior. Hyundai didn't ask me to do any publicity, but I did because I was grateful. And as of this writing, I've bought a brand-new Palisade I call "Maxine," and I love driving it.

The experience with BMW taught me something I won't forget: You better listen to that part of you that's guiding your moves. And you better read the words being said very carefully and with comprehension. Because when it comes to business, making assumptions will have you looking crazy.

I HAD A NEW CAR, so now it was time to think bigger. That's when buying a house began to seem like the obvious next move.

I started weighing my options. Did I want to rent? Maybe get a high-rise and live a soft-glam luxury life? Or did I want to own something—something in my name, with no landlord raising the rent every year? A place I could turn into an income property if life shifted again. Something I could sell, renovate, knock down walls in, and reshape however I needed. Owning meant choice and, I suppose, the stability I had always wanted. Once I looked at the money coming in and asked myself what would serve me best in the long term, the decision became clear.

I could have bought a huge home that I could grow into and spent an exorbitant amount of money. Or I could have bought a modest home that fit where I was, at a price point I was comfortable with. I chose to be true to myself. Despite the post–"Who TF Did I Marry?" success, I didn't get the biggest or most luxurious home. It was more important to me to have a home where I felt safe. I didn't need to be in the middle of the city, and I didn't need to be around a bunch of people. I just needed my own cozy space.

I cried in the car after my closing. Buying my home was exciting, but it was also terrifying. Thankfully the negotiations weren't dramatic at all. My realtor, Ashley, told me, "This is the lowest number he's willing to accept." I offered it, and within a few hours, it was accepted. That was it. Were there moments during the process when I felt triggered? Absolutely. When I walked through homes and remembered the tours Legion and I had done together, or when I saw floor plans that reminded me of the dream house he claimed he had put an offer on? Those memories would sneak in uninvited. But I kept reminding myself: *That was then. This is now.* My peace was no longer negotiable. That sounds simple enough because it is simple enough.

On closing day, I loved signing every single piece of paperwork. I didn't complain once. The seller, a white man, had bought the house as a new build with his fiancée. It was supposed to be their family home. They had broken up, and he kept the house, commuting nearly an hour and a half to work in Atlanta. Ironically, it was the same kind of commute I'd been making before. He sat with his agent, I sat with mine, and an attorney sat at the head of the table. I was the only Black person in the entire room. Every woman in that office was white. Even my mortgage specialist was a (really kind and cool) white guy. I'm painting this picture for a reason.

When I first walked in, the administrative assistant, an older Southern white woman, greeted me warmly. I assumed she was just being polite at first, but later I realized something else was happening. The women in the office knew *exactly* who I was. After the closing, they asked to take pictures with me.

If there was ever a moment when I fully understood that my story was bigger than I realized, it was that day. Grown Southern white women were telling me, "I watched all fifty parts with my daughter," or "My granddaughter told me about it and then I got hooked." As I signed the paperwork, someone, either the seller's agent or the attorney, I can't remember which, looked at me and said, "I am so proud of you." And I knew she meant it. It wasn't performative. She was genuinely rooting for me.

The seller, bless him, looked confused. His agent leaned over and whispered, "She went viral. She's kind of a celebrity." He was gracious, but if I'm being honest, I'm fairly sure part of him thought, *Damn, I should have negotiated better.*

When they slid the keys across the table, I hugged Ashley. She also told me she was proud of me, and again, I finally knew it was real. After the photos and videos, I got into the Palisade Hyundai had given me and pulled out of the parking lot. And I bawled! I drove straight to the house, walked in, and cried again. It wasn't an ugly cry. It was more the kind of tears you shed when you know you've been through something and you finally realize that you've won. *I really did this. This is mine.*

Yes, the process was stressful. Yes, there were moments I wasn't sure I'd make it to the finish line. But standing in that house with those keys is a feeling I still can't put into words. It was emotionally and spiritually liberating because I wasn't waiting on someone to tell me if I deserved it or to validate my choices. I had looked at the papers, signed my name, and realized that I didn't need anyone else's permission to start again. I'd always wanted to be a homeowner. I had just assumed I would do it with my husband.

What I'm proud of is that when I realized that part of my dream wasn't happening, I figured out that I didn't have to abandon it altogether. I edited it. I rewrote the story. Maybe the original version was: *This is our family home. My husband and I will bring the kids home from the hospital here.* But when that version didn't come to pass, I could have defaulted to giving up. I could have thought, *Well, I guess I'll just rent.* But I didn't. I said, *I'll do it myself.*

And I'm not special. The truth is, so many women do this. We hit *edit* expeditiously when things don't go as planned. We are masters of the pivot. Whether it's motherhood, moving, or buying a home, we adjust and say, *I guess I'll do it alone, and it'll be okay.*

I didn't move in immediately. I closed in early September and didn't settle in until the end of the month. I wanted to change the locks and paint first. The house was only two years old, but the previous owner hadn't touched it. When I toured it, it felt so empty, like a shell. It looked like the dream of a young couple just beginning their life, frozen in time. One bed. A small couch. Blank walls. It wasn't *bad*, it just wasn't lived in. I'd like to think it was waiting for me to turn it into a home.

Now it's cozy. That was my goal. Every person who walks in says the same thing: "Your house feels like home." That's exactly what I wanted. I wanted my home to be a place where people could breathe. Where laughter was loud, and where no one felt afraid to sit down or touch anything.

The first night actually sleeping in the home was emotional for me. I think it was because the quiet was new. I wasn't hearing sirens every five minutes like I had where I was living before. Sometimes the quiet still unnerves me, but I'm adjusting well.

And boy, has there been a lot to adjust to. I've paid property taxes, HOA fees, insurance, and, of course, my mortgage. I've learned that some things come out of escrow, which was news to me. But I'm learning as I go, and that's fine. I've also learned that I hate taking my own trash to the curb—every Tuesday, rain or shine. Trash pickup is Wednesday morning, which means I'm out there rolling that bin like clockwork. Ugh. I will never get used to that. I complain about it to everybody. I tell my mama, my friends, and my co-workers. I know it's silly, but it feels *wildly* unfair. Do I need a man just to take the trash out? Perhaps. I'm comfortable admitting that. And don't even get me started on the little home repairs I have to teach myself to do.

In addition to the newfound peace I acquired at this time in my life, buying my home felt, once again, like stability—my favorite thing in this season in my life. It hasn't given me everything I want from life, but it certainly is giving me solid ground.

What does peace look like? For me, it looks like coming home from work or from a Reesa Teesa trip, turning my alarm on, and turning Alexa on to play some music as I pour a glass of wine in my kitchen. Peace looks like sleeping in on the weekends in my king-size bed with my phone set on "Do Not Disturb" until I am ready to entertain the world. These are just some of the small examples where I give myself permission to shut down and get myself together.

And I'll be honest with you, it wasn't easy to get here. Peace had to be fought for. It had to be chosen, sometimes every single day. Because for a long time, I didn't know what peace felt like. I had grown accustomed to chaos. In my old life, drama was always humming in the background: Arguing with Legion. Crying over lies. Trying to decode truths. The mental gymnastics were exhausting, but somehow they were familiar. So when things got quiet and the drama was over, I didn't know what to do with myself. It was uncomfortable. Stillness felt like a threat.

I had to detox from the adrenaline of chaos and retrain my nervous system to respond to calm, not conflict. And that kind of healing? Whew.

Nowadays, another way I maintain my peace is by making a clear distinction between Tareasa and Reesa Teesa. Nobody in my real life calls me Reesa Teesa. They mostly call me Reesa or Tareasa. Emma, my little cousin, used to call me Teesa when she was a baby, but she doesn't really do that anymore. So when I came up with Reesa Teesa, it was just a cute little nickname for social media. But after I shared such a personal story, "Reesa Teesa" took on an identity all by itself, to the extent that some people think that's the totality of who I am. Tareasa is a complex human being with a million and one stories. Reesa Teesa is known for her marriage to a pathological liar and all that came with that. And because of the way parasocial relationships work, people think they know me when they really only know Reesa Teesa. They can only connect to me through whatever entertainment value they got from watching me on social media.

Even when I meet people for interviews, it's a little surprising how many think my name is actually Reesa. I can always tell who's an experienced journalist and who's not, because an experienced journalist will ask, "Do you prefer to be called Reesa or Tareasa?" They objectively understand the difference. And what I've often said is, "For the purposes of what we're talking about, it's fine if you say Reesa." Because, if I'm honest, sometimes I like to keep that distinction. I don't want people to confuse the two. Reesa is the storyteller and speaker who was born from Tareasa feeling like it was necessary to share her story in order to heal. Tareasa still struggles. She's still trying to pick up the pieces after her whole life was demolished. Reesa Teesa is this person who will entertain with a great story and capture your attention with her unique insight on her new phase of life. She signed with Creative Artists Agency and travels the world to speak. Tareasa is still the girl who wants to be loved well. Reesa wants to build her brand. Tareasa still wants marriage and maybe even a family.

Having millions of people follow you or recognize your face does not change what you deal with privately. A bomb went off in my life, and Tareasa is simply picking up the debris right now. She's rebuilding. And Reesa is helping her do that by showing what it looks like to live out Tareasa's wildest dreams.

I recognize that it's a blessing to be able to compartmentalize in that way—to actively work on not conflating these two parts of myself. I get to use language to separate from Reesa Teesa, to turn her off or on when I need to. It's been especially helpful when it comes to setting boundaries in business. I've actually had to say, "Okay, now that's great for Reesa, but that doesn't work for Tareasa."

Part of the way I've been able to prioritize my peace is to be very intentional about self-care. That is my new thing now, and it consists of a few different things. Periodically, I will take a weekend to put my phone on Do Not Disturb and treat myself to an entire day of just asking myself, "What do you feel like doing?" Sometimes I want to pamper myself, so I'll go and try some new healing modality or spa treatments. I've tried head spas (my new favorite) and floatation tanks and, of course, traditional massage therapy. Other times, I'll take myself out to lunch. These were things that I either didn't do before or that I put at the bottom of my to-do list because someone else's wants and needs would always take precedence over mine. Self-care for me is really about setting aside time to tend to my own needs.

Another thing I do now that I rarely did before is travel regularly. I was used to the occasional trip with friends, but it was never a thing I did on a consistent basis. Again, for me it was about work and maintaining whatever relationship I had at the time. That's where my energy went, and if I'm honest, that's what I was inadvertently taught should be my priority by the women around me. Not to mention that many of the men I dated weren't into traveling all the time, and because I felt like I needed to shrink to meet them where they were, I never explored the side of myself that longed to see the world. But now, because of Reesa Teesa, I do way more traveling than I ever did before, and it has amplified my self-care rituals tremendously. Whenever I'm in a new city for work, I'll try to build in some days when I can explore. There's a big world out there, and I want to see it one city at a time. And no, the solo travel has not all been roses and rainbows. You remember that Mexico trip. There was also a trip to Punta Cana in the Dominican Republic that was just a little too romantic for my tastes, but even those trips are beautiful lessons in gratitude and self-love. One of the things that the "Who TF Did I Marry?" series exposed was the fact that I was thirty-nine years old and had missed out on so many opportunities to see the world because I was waiting for someone to go with me. Now if I want to go somewhere, I do. If I have a long weekend coming up, like Veterans Day, I'll challenge myself. *Let's go to Seattle. Or what about Maine? I need a freaking lobster roll ASAP.* The act of giving myself permission to travel alone is part of the peace I extend myself.

There are days when I still struggle with this new way of being in the world. The fear that drove my poor decision-making before can rear its petty little head and make me think about the fact that I don't have someone sharing these trips with me. I think that might be the reason why I haven't gotten on a plane to Paris to vacation by myself, or to London, my kindred spirit city. I loved it there when I went for a planned vacation, but to go by myself? I'm still working on that. And that's okay. Part of having peace for me is recognizing where I am and doing things within my boundaries. Right now, my boundary for vacations is domestic travel. I recently took a trip to Portland, Oregon, and I was so proud of myself. I got on a plane and flew five hours away. I rented a car and learned how to drive through the city with GPS. I had a list of places I wanted to go and things I wanted to do, so I turned on my music and just drove around, enjoying the vibe. I was truly at peace that weekend. When I got back home, I said to myself, "Sweetie, you can do this. Live!" And isn't that just it? Part of finding peace in your life is accepting where you are and living the best you can within that. I don't think I'll ever shake some of those desires to be married and have children, even as I consider that maybe that season has passed. It's deeply embedded in me. But I'm unwilling to be so determined to make that dream a reality that I sacrifice my whole well-being to try and do it. What I can do, and what I am doing, is find peace in what my life looks like *now*. I can live fully in the abundance of what is and not necessarily what I wish it was.

It's incredibly important for me on this journey to not be so focused on Reesa Teesa that I forget Tareasa. I cannot be Reesa Teesa without taking care of Tareasa. And taking care of Tareasa might look like solo trips sometimes, but other times it just looks like sitting in my new comfy chair, in my new nook, reading or listening to music. Or having a heart-to-heart conversation with a friend. Or watching a Georgia football game by myself. I love my solitude, and now I know the value of it.

LET ME BE REAL: There's absolutely something addictive about chaos when you've lived in it long enough. That adrenaline rush when things are uncertain, the push and pull of drama, can start to feel like love or acceptance. But that's not real. Love is safe. And the love I now give myself is rooted in peace. I no longer need grand gestures to feel worthy. I'm not chasing the kind of excitement that costs me my sleep or my sanity. I protect my space like it's sacred, because it is. That doesn't mean I live in isolation. It just means that the people who come into my physical or emotional space have to come correct.

Even as I'm working this out for myself, I want you to know that peace is rarely passive. We don't just stumble into it. Peace is an active choice that we continue to cultivate and defend daily. This world will try to convince you that you need to keep proving yourself in order to be worthy of whatever it is your heart is seeking, but it's all a ruse. Protect your peace. Make it a practice. Say no when you want to say yes just to keep the peace outside of you. End that conversation that you know isn't going anywhere. Block that number, Sis. Yes, *you*! Unfollow people who make you doubt your progress. Most of all, be okay with being misunderstood. Why? Because you know who you are.

Prioritizing peace over these last couple of years since the series dropped has been one of the most radical and healing decisions I've ever made. My life is still full of responsibilities, deadlines, and decisions. But I don't move from a place of urgency. I move from a place of peace.

Over and over again, I've done things that could be considered declarations that I would no longer wait for someone else to hand me my healing. It started with telling my story but also with buying my home, taking solo trips, and speaking in front of an audience despite being scared out of my mind. And now that I know what peace truly feels like, I can open myself up to whatever else God has in store for me.

So ask yourself: What does peace look like for you? What or who is standing in the way of that? And what would it look like to reclaim your life with peace at the center? Because once you realize that peace is possible, you'll stop settling for anything less.

11

I Defined My Boundaries

Boundaries protect your heart and honor your truth.

CHOOSING PEACE MEANT SETTING BOUNDARIES, not just with other people but with myself. I had to be intentional about not entertaining anyone or anything that disrupts my peace. That includes people who come around only to stir up gossip or so-called friends who didn't support my healing. Even parts of me that still wanted to replay old conversations or wonder *what if*? Ugh, there are those two words again!

Clearly I wouldn't even be writing this book if I hadn't had such a hard time setting boundaries in my previous relationships, and I paid a pretty costly price for that. Boundaries were always something I *said* I had, but truthfully I didn't live them out. At my big age, I'm just now learning how to really stand on the words *No, I'm not doing that.* And to be clear, that's what boundaries are. They are the actions you are going to take (or not) in response to someone else's. It's important to make that distinction. Too many of us think telling someone what to do or how to act is setting a boundary. It isn't. Telling someone what you're going to do in response to an action is setting a boundary. I could tell a friend to stop calling me after eleven P.M., but it's not until I stop picking up the phone after eleven P.M. that I've set a boundary. My first real foray into boundary setting came along when I released "Who TF Did I Marry?" on TikTok.

The silence I experienced after ending my relationship with Legion and moving out of our shared home might have been deafening, but it was also liberating. I could finally hear myself think. I could breathe again. Eventually, I had an idea:

What if I just told my story?

It was just a whisper at first, nothing I seriously considered or planned, because I wasn't even using TikTok like that. But that whisper became a thought. That thought became a question. And that question became a conviction. It was like the peace I'd finally found gave me clarity. It showed me that there was further healing available in giving my story some air.

So I opened up TikTok and got to running my mouth.

As I've said, I wasn't trying to go viral or build a brand. I was just trying to reclaim something that had been taken from me: my voice.

The first video I made felt like a glimpse—a taste. And the internet did what the internet does: It ate it up. Then it asked for more.

I knew this story would take some time to tell, but I didn't think it would take fifty parts to tell it. With every video, I felt myself getting stronger and becoming more whole. Not because some people believed me, although that was good. Certainly not because I gained followers, though that was surreal. It was because I was no longer shrinking so that someone else could feel big. I was no longer biting my tongue so that someone else wouldn't be exposed. There was no more pretending.

But I also dealt with the evil side of things. Some people didn't believe me. Others laughed at my pain. There were plenty of people who had the audacity to call me stupid and weak from behind their keyboards. So much of my story, when it comes to relationships, has been about what the other person wanted. Now it's about what Tareasa wants. And that's a huge deal. So every time I felt fear creeping up my spine, I asked myself again: *What do you want to do?* And the answer was always the same: *Tell the truth.*

Tell the truth so someone else won't feel alone. Tell the truth so someone else can recognize the red flags. Tell the truth because secrets protect abusers, and silence is their weapon. I told it all, not because I wanted pity but because I wanted freedom.

Going viral on social media has a way of slapping you upside the head and showing you the ugly side of notoriety. People love to say they'd trade places with you in a heartbeat, until they realize that being "known" means being known by strangers who will gladly project their pain onto you. I've been very vocal about the toll it can take on your mental health, but I don't really know that I've found a way to effectively handle the parasocial dynamic that comes along with it. I've had to learn to set boundaries as I go. Social media is truly out of hand nowadays, and whatever boundaries I set for myself, they have to exist under an umbrella of something larger that applies both offline and on. At first my boundaries were mostly about protecting my mental health. When the story went viral, there was a lot of backlash. People in the comments called me everything but a child of God. It is difficult when you see strangers posting think pieces about you as if they know you. It is even more heartbreaking to realize that you opened Pandora's box just because you told your story. From that experience, the first boundary I set involved deciding not to read the comments. As hard as that is to do, I learned early on that if I sat and read the comments for too long, scrolling through a never-ending rabbit hole of strangers dissecting my story as if I were a fictional character, I would end up in tears, or incredibly pissed off. "She should've known better." "Ain't no way that happened." "She's lying for clout." Those words sting, even when I know better than to take them to heart. But my boundary setting had to start right there.

Interestingly enough, Beavis and Washington Monument (aka WM) had no idea I had put the story out or that it was going viral.

From what I understand, WM found out through his niece. She said something like, "I'm watching this thing on social media, and this girl is telling her story about her crazy ass ex." He didn't know what she was talking about, so she showed him a clip. That's how he found out. Apparently, everyone else in his family had already been talking about the series, but he had no idea it had gotten as big as it did.

Beavis found out through a woman he was dating. She was watching the series, told him about it, and showed him a clip, and he said, "Oh my God, I know her."

Their reactions were very different. WM checked in. Especially when the backlash started. I think he was a bit upset at first, but once he got a fuller picture of how bad the situation with Legion really was, he stopped giving me a hard time. He called me and said, "I'm not calling to give you some dick, I just want to know how you are doing." His checking in meant a lot to me.

Beavis, on the other hand, felt strongly that I shouldn't have said anything at all. He's not a fan of social media, and he believed that the backlash was my fault. His stance was essentially *You opened your mouth, so whatever you're getting, you brought it on yourself.*

One night, my mother overheard me on the phone with him and snapped a little. She told him, "As her friend, you need to support her. Whether you agree with it or not, this is her experience. This is her story to tell. You don't tell someone to keep their mouth shut about something they've lived through." My mom felt a way about the fact that he was even remotely negative about it.

For the most part, though, I went through the backlash alone. Not because people didn't care but because I didn't pull people into it. In a way, that's another boundary I set for myself. I guess I could have pulled in more people who loved and cared for me to help me navigate all that was being thrown my way. Maybe it would have helped me shed fewer tears. But I truly believed the situation was temporary. I kept telling myself *This too shall pass.* One thing I understood about social media was that the backlash would eventually die down. But while it lasted, it was ugly and constant. I held on to the scripture that says, "Weeping may endure for a night, but joy comes in the morning"—though I remember thinking, and even posting on Facebook, *But damn, how long is this night?*

One of my new mottos has become *I'm not even entertaining that.* That sentence alone has saved my peace more than I can explain. Because here's the truth: Boundaries are not for other people. They're for me. They protect my sanity, my peace, and even my sense of self. So no, I'm not going to respond to negative comments or videos about me. Not because I don't want accountability but because the cost is too high. I'm not willing to play with my well-being, and I have enough people around me whom I trust to help me remain accountable. Plus I've already told my story: the good, bad, and embarrassing parts. And I owned all of it. I already know what I could've done better; to engage in back-and-forth arguments with people I'll never meet is something I am *just not doing.* That ain't arrogance; that's wisdom.

Because social media is the vehicle people used to get to know me, it is very difficult to turn that fire hydrant of commentary off once it's on. Especially when you didn't even know you had turned it on in the first place. Some days it seems like the only real option to take back control is to disappear from social media. When the world is watching, sometimes you have to shut it off just to hear your own voice again.

But there's a catch. If I'd disappeared from the internet because of those comments, many of the opportunities I've gotten would have never found me. The truth is, time is money in this world. You must be continually "hot" in order to make a living. That's the dilemma. The only true way to have your boundaries honored in these content creator streets is to literally cut off the monster.

The one decision I have made, and the one I'm really planning to stick to, is to not be a full-time content creator—mostly because I don't think that's my niche anyway. I'm a storyteller. That's it. In a world where you are hot one week and cold the next, the only thing I can do for myself is stay as authentic as possible, and that means accepting that I'm not willing to do whatever it takes to go viral and be all over people's For You page. If it happens organically like it did the first time, so be it. But it won't be because I manufactured something to make virality happen.

Boundaries started as damage control. Now they are slowly but surely becoming a form of healing. They apply to everything: friendships, finances, relationships, even how I spend my time.

I define a healthy boundary as *anything that protects me:* mentally, emotionally, financially, physically, even sexually. Those boundaries are very specific to Tareasa. And I use the word *anything* intentionally because what protects me might look completely different from what protects you. My boundaries are shaped by pain, growth, self-awareness, and yes, sometimes by trial and error.

So many people on the internet swore I made a bunch of money off the TikTok series alone. Folks were convinced I walked away with $100,000 just from TikTok's Creator Fund, as if the moment the videos went viral a bag had fallen into my lap. But the truth? I've made less than $5,000 from that. Less. Than. Five. Thousand. Dollars.

What I *did* get, almost immediately, was attention from brands, companies, and people circling closer than I was comfortable with. It felt like some of them saw me as an easy mark—a woman who had been naive and might still be naive. And I could feel the unspoken question hovering in the air: *Is she still dumb?*

For a while, it was clear I wasn't being taken seriously. So I started dropping the name of my attorney. That's when the tone shifted. That's when people realized I wasn't operating alone, and I wasn't guessing my way through this.

Yes, opportunities came. There were perks, conversations, and rooms I never imagined I'd enter. I sat on couches at *Good Morning America* and *Tamron Hall*. My lawyer even told me that my earning potential was astronomical. And I received that information with gratitude but also with both feet planted firmly on the ground.

That's because I know viral fame is fragile. I've seen the evidence of it. One minute, everyone knows your name. The next minute, they are scrolling past you like you're yesterday's news. So for now, I've kept my nine-to-five. I choose not to romanticize this moment, because I've seen how quickly it can turn. As fast as this came, it can leave you flat—with no job, no money, and no friends.

Just vibes and screenshots of you smiling on TV. And that's not real security, which I suppose is still what I long for.

This is why I'm intentional about how I spend. A healthy financial boundary for me looks like restraint. I do not just go and splurge. I love self-care days, but I've learned to limit them to once a month. I love to travel, but I do it smartly and plan trips around holidays so I don't have to take too much time off work. Labor Day weekend, Veterans Day weekend—that's my travel rhythm. I know that may sound weird, but I try to use my paid time off for actual mental health days as well as comped Reesa Teesa things.

I also manage my money with those boundaries in mind. Instead of spending a bunch of money using my credit card, I'll cash in my Delta miles for flights and rental cars (so I don't waste money on Ubers). Instead of staying at a five-star hotel, I'll do a cost comparison and stay at a five-star Airbnb. These might sound like small things, but they're boundaries that keep me from slipping into old habits of overextending myself like I did when I first started making more money. Let's just say I went a little crazy. I was never a shopaholic, but it was nice to think, *Oh, I'm going to get new work clothes, and I'm not looking at the total.* Then there was a solo trip I took in April 2024 to Key Largo, Florida. I went to this place called the Bungalows, and my tab for the week I stayed there was about $7,000. Now Reesa Teesa might have had a ball that week, but Tareasa knew damn well that didn't make no sense. No matter how you slice it, I should not have spent that much money on one solo trip. Nowadays I try to use more wisdom, as I've come to believe that financial discipline is an act of self-respect.

I also have emotional boundaries—or maybe they are more like relational boundaries. Those have been much harder to hold. My rule now is simple: I don't give more than what I'm given. In the past, I've been guilty of pouring myself into people with no reciprocation. And obviously, the cost of all that pouring was being left empty. So I've chosen not to do that anymore. No more one-sided friendships where I'm calling or texting or checking in more than the other person does. I get that sometimes people have things going on in their lives that prevent them from reaching out. There are plenty of people I know who struggle with depression or who just don't have the time, energy, and bandwidth to be who they need to be at a particular moment. That doesn't mean they don't care. But that isn't everybody. In some cases, folks were not used to having to make an effort with me, because I had never required them to. It had gotten to a point where, when I found myself being absolutely dogged out all over the internet, one of my so-called best friends never even bothered to pick up the phone to see how I was doing. So that was it for me. Reciprocity matters. I'm going to match whatever someone is putting into our relationship. If you call me, I'm going to call you. It may not be every day, and that is okay, because we do have our own lives to live, but you will hear from me. Why? Because I hear from you, and I care enough to show you that effort in return.

I have people in my life who I have been friends with for years, and truth be told, it has been months since we've talked. The only time I hear from these friends is when they respond to me reaching out, and I'm honestly tired of that. So I told myself when I turned forty that I wasn't doing that anymore. Yes, people have lives, and they are busy; that's understandable. But also, like Maya Angelou said, I've taught people how to treat me. The expectation was always for me to reach out. How much do you actually value me if our entire friendship is dependent upon me reaching out to you?

So setting a healthy boundary for me now means no longer always being the one to initiate contact—and being okay with what that might mean. Going forward, I don't want to do all the work in my relationships. I want to be around people who are willing to share that emotional and mental labor.

It is fucking exhausting to always be giving and to be getting nothing in return—to be in a dark place and have none of the people who claimed to love you checking on you or bringing any light. I know some people will say, "Oh, she's feeling herself, that's why she's not calling." No, it is not that at all. It's mostly because, damn it, I need somebody to check on me too! If everything depends on me reaching out, that's not a friendship; it's a performance.

I've joked with friends, saying, "Listen, I'm not Kobe. I cannot carry the Lakers by myself." Maybe that's me making light of it, but I mean it. When it comes to relationships, it's exhausting to be the one carrying the team. Like any other human, I want and need someone checking on me just as I check on others. I want to hear someone genuinely ask me how I'm doing and be willing to wait around for the answer.

Having these relational boundaries has helped me tremendously with having healthy mental boundaries. They go hand in hand. I've carried that kind of mental load in my relationships before, and I choose not to do so anymore. For instance, every night at nine o'clock, my phone automatically turns on a setting I've named *Time to Rest*. From nine P.M. to eight A.M., I am not taking phone calls or answering text messages or emails unless they are work-related. And even with work or Reesa Teesa stuff, I'm selective. That's my time to breathe.

Of course, if my family needs to break through the setting because of an emergency, they can, but this is one way I give myself the mental space to reset and refresh every day. I've even begun to test "going dark" on my self-care days or on my commutes to work. That means I'm not available for the chitchat and I'm focused on getting my mind ready for what's to come in my day. It's not that anything is wrong when I do this. I just need space. That time belongs to me.

There are some days when I talk to my mom after work. That's important to me; it's a kind of therapy if I'm being honest. But lately I've even slowed down on doing that. It's not because I don't want to talk to her but more because I need to get still and exhale from the day. I may listen to music or an audiobook or sit in silence. It might sound small, but these routines I'm establishing are sacred and part of my healing process. They allow me to recharge in a way that even the most pleasant and life-giving interactions cannot. Setting these boundaries lets me reclaim my time from a world that always wants access to me.

Friend, you can't keep pouring into people who let you drown. You don't have to chase people to prove your loyalty. That's not bitterness either. It's balance. Boundaries don't just apply to relationships; they reveal them. The people who truly love and respect you will honor your limits without making you feel guilty. I used to think being available for the people in my life all the time was a sign of love. Now I know it's a setup for burnout.

ROMANTIC BOUNDARIES, THOUGH? Those are still a work in progress. I wish I could say I've got it all figured out, but I don't. Like many women, I was taught that if a guy is really into you, he's going to put forth the effort. Well, in my situation, Legion did put forth the effort in the beginning, but I still misread the intentions behind that effort. So now I have to take it a step further. I have to look for not only effort but so much more.

I know that most of the boundaries I set now are about protecting myself. I'm doing certain things out of fear versus some extreme love for myself. The truth is that my boundaries with men lately have been more about fear than love. I tell myself that I'm protecting my heart from the pain of my past, but sometimes what I'm really doing is building walls to ensure that people can't hurt me. I'm rarely entertaining blind dates. I'm not spending hours and hours on the phone with somebody new. But part of me feels like I'm doing what I have to do to heal. Those fearful boundaries, those walls, are giving me the time and space to learn how to love myself for real, for real.

Funnily enough, this lesson was driven home to me recently during my own movie-worthy "meet cute" moment.

I had to go to an awards event for work. At the bar, I was sitting with a couple I know. The husband works with me, but his wife and I always act like cousins whenever we get together. We're all laughing and having a good time when I look down the bar and see this fine, muscular guy staring at me. I recognized him from the banquet we'd been at earlier.

Me being me, I couldn't resist joking with him. "You really gon' eat all that food in front of you? Couldn't even offer a sista a cheeseburger?"

He laughed. We gave each other our names, and it turned out he worked for an agency in Metro Atlanta. By this time, my friend's wife was already hyping us up, saying, "Oh my God, this is kismet."

I guess.

Let's call him Casper. That whole evening, Casper and I talked and joked with each other, and by the end of the night, we were saying that we'd have to come back to this hotel and get married one day, since it's where we met. Before we said good night, he gave me a hug that made me melt. I remember it to this day.

Listen, I was determined to stay on the straight and narrow. *I'm not gon' be a hoe tonight. Nope, nope, nope. I'm on a healing journey.*

We exchanged numbers, and he never called. Not even a single text.

And guess what Reesa did?

I deleted his number.

Simple as that.

No ruminating on why. No letting my emotions carry me away with some narrative that may or may not be true.

Fast-forward to a few months later, and my agency held an event that was attended by folks in his agency. I walked in sweating because it was hot as hell. It was also the day after Beyoncé's Renaissance concert, and I was wearing a jersey, jeans, a ponytail, and sunglasses in order to hide my red and tired eyes. I was just trying to survive the day, okay? And as soon as I turned the corner, there he was: Casper.

He walked up to me, gave me the Baptist church side hug, and said, "Hey, I don't hear from you."

I took my sunglasses off, looked him dead in the face, and said, "I deleted your number."

Casper looked stunned. I'm certain he was not used to women setting boundaries.

"You did what?!" he exclaimed.

"I deleted your number. You asked for mine and never used it. Obviously you weren't interested. But hey, it's good to see you." I patted him on the shoulder and walked off.

By the time I got back to my car, I had received two text messages from him with his work and his personal phone numbers.

CASPER: This is my number. Please lock it in. Don't delete it.

Hmmm.

So Casper and I started talking. I appreciated the fact that he was consistent. He called me three times a day: on his way to work, on his lunch break, and after work. Eventually, he asked me out.

Well, technically he said it was a dinner "amongst friends." *Okay, fine.* I wore a dress and four-inch heels—call it what you want.

Our first date was amazing. We laughed. Talked. Connected more. The second date was more of the same thing. That is, until he hit me with the "I'm scared we'll mess up our friendship. I just wanna be friends."

Record scratch.

Casper was telling me this while holding my hand at a romantic Italian restaurant.

After taking some time to think, I texted him the next day.

"Thank you for your honesty. But I didn't sign up to be your friend. I really liked you. I thought there was something mutual here. But clearly we want different things, so I'm taking myself out of the equation."

Of course, he responded with "Oh my God, I'm so hurt" and a bunch of other nonsense.

But I was proud of myself. I set a boundary. I didn't fall into the old Tareasa trap of *let me convince him to want me.* I'd played that game before. (Got the T-shirts and the medals.) I'm not playing anymore.

You might be thinking, *Isn't friendship what you wanted, Tareasa?*

Yes, absolutely. But the mixed signals were the problem. Casper really wanted a situationship. That whole *You do you, I do me, but let's do each other* thing. I wasn't interested. And because he follows me on Facebook, he now knows all about the Reesa Teesa stuff, which I'm sure has shocked him. After a long hiatus, we went out to eat last year, and you can imagine just how completely different the vibe was. Mostly because *I'm* different. He didn't know what to make of that, because I was chill and on some "How you been? How's life? How are the kids?" kind of thing. I had no butterflies and certainly no illusions.

"Where's the woman who was interested in me?" he asked when I saw him.

I looked at him, once again, dead in the face and said, "She disappeared a while ago. Life is very different for me now." I'm proud of that moment. It was a small victory for a woman who is learning every day to choose herself.

Yes, Casper is still handsome. But I'm not playing that game anymore. I know what I want. I know how to set boundaries. I know now that exiting stage left when someone can't meet you where you are is totally okay. I smile sometimes when I think about him, not because of what could've been but because he is a reminder that I know how to choose me.

Right now, I'm not in a space where I can be fully vulnerable with anyone new. I poured so much of myself into the "Who TF Did I Marry?" series that I feel like I've already handed the world a piece of my soul. That kind of vulnerability takes something out of you. The series was the full extent of emotional vulnerability I could give, and that was tremendous.

When people ask, "So, are you dating again?" I laugh. As I've said previously, I am only comfortable hanging out with someone as friends right now. We can have a good time, but in the end, we will go our separate ways. I'm good with a text or a call occasionally—one where we catch up and talk about platonic things. But that's it. I am certainly *not* comfortable with getting dressed up to go on a date where I will interrogate some stranger or be interrogated by one. I'm not comfortable with all the *what do you bring to the table?* questions, and I'm even less comfortable with the answers.

That word *comfortable* is how I'm navigating the dating world and establishing boundaries right now: What makes me comfortable? There was a time after my divorce when I did not know what I was comfortable with and was wildin' a little bit. I had no clue what I could or could not accept. But that's different now. I can put it into words. I can articulate what it is that I like and what it is that I don't.

I am not a fan of a guy who texts me, "Good morning, beautiful, grand rising," and all that bullshit. Nope, I'm good. I do love a "Hey, you remember when we were talking about such and such last night? I was thinking . . ." When conversation feels like a man running game, you can be sure Tareasa is running away. I'm more comfortable when the energy feels genuine. I'm all in on regular degular human interaction.

If I do decide to go on a date with a man and every joke he makes is sexual, I now have no problem letting him know he crossed a boundary—or even walking away from the date and him entirely. I said this exact thing to Casper after his declaration for friendship. Every joke he made was about sex. And I told him I wasn't interested in that type of friendship. I'm just not. It is very apparent to me that you have one thing on your mind, and while we are both grown and you're free to talk about whatever you want to talk about, it's not interesting to me. He swore up and down it wasn't like that, said he'd still be my friend and check on me. Spoiler alert: He didn't.

Eventually Casper messaged me: "Why don't I ever hear from you?"

"The answer is simple," I messaged back. "Because I never hear from you."

Whew! Boundaries make the truth plain.

It's not as if I haven't thought about what it would require for me to take down my walls and consider a long-term relationship. I think the biggest indicator of my readiness to move forward would be how the person makes me feel. And no, I don't mean the butterflies of attraction and the heart-eyed infatuation. I mean, *Do I feel safe with this person?* Not just physically safe but emotionally safe. Are the green flags plentiful versus the raging red ones? Is this a person whose actions and history are matching what they're saying and what they've promised? When they say that they're going to do something, do they do it? Is honesty their first nature?

Emotional safety, for me, is when I am able to confide in my partner. When I know they are not a human filing cabinet, storing away the things I share with them only to use them against me later in an argument or conflict (see: Dallas). I want someone who has seen me in all four seasons, as the saying goes. Someone who has seen me raging and grieving and overjoyed and self-conscious and still never throws any of that back in my face.

On that same note, the person I would consider having a long-term relationship with now would have to be someone who can tell me about myself with kindness and compassion. Do I feel safe enough with this person to allow them to tell me the flaws that they see? Can I receive criticism from them because I know it's coming from a place of wanting me to be my best self and not a desire to put me down? And can I disagree with this person and not have it taken as a personal attack?

In so many of my relationships, I carried a deep fear of disagreement. I knew one argument could cause me to mentally spiral. I'd find myself saying, over and over, "Oh my God, what did I do wrong?" I suppose part of the reason why setting these hard boundaries is necessary for me right now is because I know myself. I know that my love language is quality time, but I also know that my desire for quality time is tied to the fact that I have an anxious attachment style. The moment a guy leaves my presence, my brain starts going a hundred miles an hour. The stories about what he might be doing or feeling start ramping up, and they don't stop until he is physically near me again. It's the same thing with arguments. One conflict, and I was spiraling into self-doubt and fear. While that's my anxious attachment style showing up, it's also stemming from my insecurity about losing what I thought I was building with these men. But many times, it was *also* the very real threats and manipulation I experienced from them.

It's interesting that my issues with anxious attachment tend to only show up in romantic relationships—and specifically with someone I genuinely care about. As I've alluded to throughout this book, I tend to dive headfirst into those kinds of relationships, which is something I'm less likely to do in friendships or at work. My mind loves to race ahead of my reality. Of course, this anxious attachment doesn't appear in every interaction I have with men. It almost exclusively arises once a connection turns romantic, and especially after being intimate. That's when the fear and doubt start creeping in, and I start worrying and overthinking.

Let's be real: It is very easy for people to say, "Well, shit, don't hold your tongue. If they want to leave after you've said your piece, let them leave." But how many times do we avoid confrontation because we don't want to deal with the aftermath? Probably more often than any of us will admit. I know for a fact that this is connected to the lack of emotional safety in our relationships. We call it "keeping the peace," but it's really about keeping ourselves safe (at least in our minds).

I guess this means I need a steadfast person. A committed person. Someone who, when we disagree, never hits below the belt. Someone who I can have an argument with and not be afraid the relationship is over. The realest thing is, I've never known what that feels like. I don't know what it's like to be with a partner who, even on the bad days, is still there with me. I've always experienced the manipulation of "Fuck it, we don't have to be together then!" And the fear and loneliness that comes with that.

I know that balanced relationships where both parties implement healthy conflict resolution strategies exist, but I have never experienced one. So that's what I would need to see. I'm doing my work now, and I need him—whoever he is—to do his. These green flags are the only way I'd consider dipping my toe back into the dating pool.

Another huge transition point for me will be when I can focus on the green flags more than the red. Yes, I will continue to pay attention to the red flags. I've missed too many in my life to ever stop. But I recognize that always looking for the negative means that I will likely only find the negative. I could also run the risk of conjuring up red flags that aren't there because I've been so hurt in the past. That will take some time and healing though. I'm still working on deciphering whether I'm overthinking a situation or seeing something that's truly there. Add the overthinking to the awareness of my attachment style, and it explains why it's difficult for me to parse out the green and red flags. I don't know the difference right now, and that is why I feel like the best thing is to be alone until I do.

In addition to paying attention to things that are harmful, I want to be able to get to a point where I'm noticing the green flags. I want to be in a situation where the green flags of honesty and respect are flying so wildly and with abandon that I couldn't ignore them if I wanted to. That's important to me, because I've had too many men see my triggers and do everything in their power to step right on the land mines of my emotions. They get a kick out of breaching those boundaries. Either that or they wave off my feelings like they are no big deal and not worthy of respect. A huge green flag for me? Respecting my boundaries. If a man knows something is triggering for me and makes a strong and concerted effort to steer clear of it, that's a green flag. They are conscious of something that is painful, and they are working to not disrupt things. They respect who I am and what I've been through, and they care enough to be mindful. Now that's sexy!

Here's what I tell my friends when they ask how to start setting their own boundaries: "Start by asking yourself what you're comfortable with." Write it out if you must. But never feel any guilt about your boundaries. You do not have to apologize for doing what you need to do. For staying within your comfort zone. And if you don't know your boundaries yet, that's okay too. There was a time after my divorce when I couldn't have answered that question either. Healing takes time, and clarity comes with it. Once you start to name what feels safe and what doesn't, you'll begin to see your boundaries taking shape.

If you're comfortable going out with a guy but you're not ready to invite him over, then meet him at a restaurant. Drive your own car. Protect your space. You don't owe anyone an explanation for doing what keeps you emotionally safe, and you are not obligated to make yourself available to people who haven't earned that access. Listen, even if you're not sure what your boundaries are yet, honoring that is still a boundary. *Not knowing* is part of the process. Time, I've found, is both a healer and a teacher. It will show you what deserves your yes and what requires your no. If anything, boundaries have given me the space to see clearly—to separate who genuinely cares from who just wants proximity to my pain.

One day, these boundaries turned walls will soften into gates for me. And maybe, just maybe, those gates will turn into open doors. But until then, I choose not to see my boundaries or walls as barriers that keep love out. I see them as bridges that allow the *right* kind of love in. Yes, they can sometimes *feel* like a fortress around my heart, but I know deep down that they are not. Boundaries are reminders that peace isn't something that just happens because little Tareasa once imagined she'd have some great love one day. It happens because grown Tareasa took the time to heal her broken heart. Maybe one day I'll let someone close enough to see that my fortress isn't made of stone so much as it's made of lessons. But for now, I'm content knowing that every no I speak is clearing the path for a more intentional yes.

12

I Honored My Truth

Living authentically is the key to real freedom.

I DIDN'T GROW UP DREAMING ABOUT standing on stages. I wasn't the little girl lining up her dolls and giving speeches, nor did I imagine that one day I'd be flown across the country to share some life-altering truth about myself in a room full of industry leaders. In fact, if you had asked me even a year before my appearance at CAA Amplify whether I saw myself speaking publicly on behalf of my own experiences, I would have laughed and told you that's not my lane. But the truth has a way of chasing you down. It will tap you on the shoulder, and if you don't respond after its nudge, it will show up in front of you with a microphone in its hand, saying, *We're doing this now.*

After "Who TF Did I Marry?" went viral, I got a DM from a woman who worked with someone at BET.

"We've been watching your story," she said. "Someone here wants to talk to you." Eventually I gave her my phone number, and the person who called me was Kenya Barris—yes, the writer, director, and producer of *Black-ish*. This was literally within two weeks of me uploading the series. He got straight to it.

"We love this story. We want to buy the rights and develop it into a TV show."

All of it sounded amazing. Then he asked me a simple question: "Do you have an attorney?"

I told him the truth. "No. I just uploaded a story. I don't have anybody."

"First things first: You need an entertainment attorney. Whoever that is, that's who we'll negotiate with," he said. He then outlined exactly how the process would work if I decided to sell the rights to BET. I'll always be grateful to Kenya for telling me that.

So I did the only thing I knew to do. I Googled *entertainment attorneys in Atlanta*. Maybe even *Black entertainment attorneys in Atlanta*. I ended up with three names. I called all three and left them voicemails. I said something very vague like, "Hi, my name is Tareasa Johnson. I went viral on social media and may have a potential deal coming up. I need legal representation."

Within minutes, one attorney called me back: Olivia Harris. She hadn't even heard the voicemail yet. She just saw a missed call and returned it. She had no idea who I was and knew nothing about a fifty-part TikTok series. But I explained the situation: "I spoke with someone at BET, and they told me I need an entertainment attorney."

I looked her up while we were on the phone. Twenty-plus years of experience. A Spelman grad. *Okay, okay. She knows her shit.*

While I was driving down I-75, headed to work, she said, "I'm sending you a document that allows me to negotiate on your behalf. I need you to sign it as soon as possible so I can start speaking to BET." I sent her the contact information for everyone I'd been communicating with, and then I pulled over just before the Forest Park exit. I opened the document on my phone, electronically signed it right there on the side of the highway, and sent it back.

She said, "Okay. I'm your attorney now. I'll handle the conversations."

What I understand now, though I didn't fully understand it then, is that BET was trying to move too quickly—which makes sense. They were trying to get in before anyone else could. Once Olivia stepped in, though, everything shifted. As the story kept growing, I started receiving more DMs, and for the first time, I could say, "I have an attorney."

As I said before, when it came to boundaries, the game changed the moment people realized Reesa Teesa had legal representation. I genuinely believe some folks assumed I was just a random woman who went viral and didn't know anything. I mean, I did say in the series that I was living paycheck to paycheck. They probably thought they could offer me a few thousand dollars and I'd take it. What BET initially offered was nowhere near the money I eventually signed for. They lowballed me, and my attorney shut it down immediately.

After *Good Morning America,* everything changed again. The response from the public shifted. Before that, social media was full of comments calling me stupid, desperate, and not worth watching. Afterward, the tide turned, and more people who identified with what I was going through voiced their support.

BET wouldn't budge on the money they had offered, so Olivia explained to me that I would likely need an agent. While she can review contracts and do some negotiating, a well-connected agent can open doors. They can put your name in rooms you can't access alone.

So I met with three agencies: CAA, UTA, and the WME Group. I knew they were the top three agencies in Hollywood, but honestly, I wasn't nervous. It was made very clear to me: *They want you.* So I figured I just needed to go in and let them sell themselves. I met with all three over Zoom during a two-day span. UTA had three or four people on the call. WME had two. CAA had nine.

Nine people, each representing a different branch: scripted, unscripted, publishing, podcasts, speaking, brand deals. They had Black people on the call. People of color. And they had a plan. They already knew about BET. They laid out exactly what they saw for me across every space.

And the thing that sealed it? They spoke plainly. No big, confusing industry jargon. It felt like they were saying, "We want you. AND here's how serious we are."

I was in New York at the time, taking all these meetings from my hotel room alongside Olivia. When we finished, she asked, "What do you think?"

I said, "It's CAA. No question."

They sent the paperwork over and I signed it again. Then the press release went out. That was my first time ever being part of a press release. Seeing my name, my face, my story . . . *Reesa Teesa signs with CAA* . . . was surreal. It was the first time I realized that by honoring my truth and being willing to tell my story, unfiltered and without apology, I had placed myself in a realm beyond anything I could ever imagine.

And they weren't joking either. Once I signed with CAA, the doors flung wide open. My inbox was overflowing. *Google wants to work with you. TikTok has something for you.* I went from feeling invisible to feeling undeniable. Signing with CAA gave legitimacy to my brand, to *me*. This wasn't a social media agency. This wasn't mom-and-pop. It was fucking CAA. And just like that, whatever negotiations were happening with BET stopped. Because CAA brought the energy of *If you're not coming correct for our client, don't come at all. We won't even text her for $10,000.*

You can imagine that when I was invited to speak at CAA Amplify in 2024, I had no idea what that was, nor did I know what to expect. I would later learn that it is an invitation-only gathering of cultural and business changemakers who are looking to support dialogue and action that positively impacts marginalized groups. *Um, okay.* I still wasn't exactly sure what it was all about. The team at CAA kept saying, "We'll send you a video from the previous year so you can see what it is, but you must get on that stage and tell your story." When they finally sent over the footage from the year before, I watched the clip on my phone while lying across my bed. It was a beautifully produced event held at a breathtaking resort in California, where person after person stepped onstage to share amazing, polished stories with inspirational messages about identity and resilience. Some were confident and fascinating; others I couldn't connect to as much. But they were *all seasoned.* I can't lie; I was so lost. I wondered, *Why in the world do y'all want me to speak?*

Imposter syndrome reared its head something awful. It climbed into my spirit before I could even pack my suitcase. It whispered ugly nothings like: *They made a mistake. They don't realize you're not one of them. You don't belong in that environment.* To make matters worse, the summit was held all the way in Ojai, California, and I couldn't bring anybody with me—so I would be there by myself. No friends. No family. No emotional support.

When I landed in California, the sun was setting behind the mountains in that picturesque California way that makes you feel like you've arrived on the set of a movie somebody forgot to inform you that you were starring in. The resort was stunning, with lush trees and soft light. Everything was clearly expensive, but it pretended to be effortless. When I stepped into the lobby, everywhere I looked were clusters of people hugging, laughing, and greeting each other like old college friends at a reunion. It felt like walking into a cafeteria at a new school with your tray. Everyone's talking, and you don't know where to sit. I scanned the room for someone I knew—and all the faces were familiar, because many were celebrities or high-profile people. Unfortunately, I knew no one except my agent. Thank God she was there. If I had not seen her in that sea of strangers, I might have turned around and called a driver to take me back to the airport. But even with her presence, the feeling that I was in the wrong place lingered. That nagging voice: *You do not belong here.*

If I'm honest, I was angry about being in that position. I know now that this is just my way of dealing with my fear. I often try to avoid awkward situations like these because I don't like how they make me feel. But if I can't avoid them, I almost have to get angry in order to push myself through them instead of cowering. At one point, I went back to my room, got on the phone with my people, and repeated what those voices in my head were telling me: *I don't know why I'm here. I don't know anyone.* There I was, thirty-nine years old, sitting in a beautiful room at a beautiful resort, wanting to cry—all because people knew of me, but I didn't know anyone.

I texted Olivia first and said, "I want to come home." Immediately she called me and said, "What's going on? What's going on?"

I explained to her that I've spent most of my life avoiding uncomfortable situations. Ever since high school, I've hated feeling like the odd one out. So I told her plainly, "I'm ready to go. I want to come home."

I also talked to my mom and my aunt. They had been responding to the pictures and videos I was sending with things like, "Oh my God, it's so beautiful. How does it feel?" All I could say was, "I don't know why I'm here."

Of course, my mother went straight into mama mode. "Girl, it'll be fine. They brought you there for a reason. You told your story. Stand on it."

My best friend said, "It's gorgeous. I just hate that you can't bring someone with you."

But no one really gave me a *You were made for this. You know who you are. Go out there and own it* speech. The overall message was more like, "If you don't shut up and enjoy this trip, meet some people, and have a good time . . ."

Olivia was different though. She was all business.

"I don't understand why they didn't let me come with you. I could have worked that room." She was frustrated that I was there alone, especially since I was new to all of this. She felt like my scripted agents at CAA should have let her travel with me. Olivia had zero problems talking to people. I'm like that too, but only in certain situations—and definitely not there.

I texted one of my agents directly and said, "I don't know why I'm here." He responded, "Reesa, you're going to be fine. Trust me. This is a big deal. Michelle Obama is going to be there."

Okay, I thought. *At least I might meet Michelle Obama.*

Still, there were no *put your big-girl panties on and go out there* pep talks from anyone, and for a while, the desire to pack up and go home was intense.

Funnily enough, the encouragement I eventually did get came from the hair and makeup room. The women doing my hair and makeup, Black women, noticed my nerves. And I told them I was a bit scared. "Girl, don't be nervous," they said. "You're going to do amazing. We watched your story. You have changed the game. Just tell your truth."

Then one of them said something that shifted things for me: "Just act like you're talking to us."

That moment was pure sisterhood, and I'll never forget it.

After dinner that first night, I sat on the edge of my bed staring at the itinerary like it was written in a language I didn't yet understand. *I have to speak here. I have to go up on a stage and talk to these people.* "Terrified" doesn't even begin to describe the feeling. And of course, the whole time, the team at CAA was sending gentle reminders: "Whenever you're ready, we'd love to see your written speech." Written speech? I had none. I could not produce one to save my life. My mind was blank. Frozen.

Before I even arrived at Amplify, my agent had offered to suggest people to work with on storytelling. "You're so amazing, Reesa. This person will just help you get your ideas and thoughts organized." But that was the problem. I didn't know what I was going to talk about. I did have one truth I could hold on to though. Community had carried my story further than any algorithm ever could. This community I'd created online had held up my story and shared it. They let me know just how powerful support can be. My story was resonating everywhere, and I realized my community was much bigger than I had ever imagined. It was certainly bigger than TikTok. It was bigger than social media. It wasn't just think pieces written by Black women. Black men were writing about it. White women. White men. Women of color. Everybody had something to say.

I knew the story was huge when I started getting tagged in videos where people weren't even speaking English. I had no idea what they were saying, but I understood *Reesa Teesa*. I saw videos where people had translated the series into their native language.

And while I knew I wanted to talk about community at Amplify, my real moment of revelation happened later. In June 2024, I went to London with Shawn. London is a whole vibe, and we were having a ball. We went to dinner at a place called the Hippodrome, and before we sat down to eat, I went to the restroom.

I was washing my hands, drying them, and just enjoying the moment when a group of girls came in, laughing and having a good time. One of them, who I believe was Indian, caught my eye in the mirror. She said, "Oh my God, are you Reesa Teesa?"

I turned around and said, "Yeah."

The woman said, "Oh my God, it is so good to meet you."

Before that trip, I had seen videos of the series playing on televisions in local shops overseas, with people filming screens and tagging me on TikTok. Seeing that was one thing. But this was my first experience of being recognized in another country by someone who looked nothing like me.

That's when I knew. *Yeah, honey, this is bigger than you thought.*

You don't really understand how big TikTok and social media are until you leave the United States. Until you cross an ocean and realize people know who you are, because the internet truly connects the world.

At another point while in London, Shawn and I were walking down the street when a Black man approached me. He was polite and calm but excited. "Oh my God, you're Reesa," he said in a thick British accent.

Once again, I said, "Yeah."

Before I could even respond, he pulled out his phone and took a selfie.

That's when I fully grasped what community really means—the possibilities of it. I had my people. Those I am close to. Friends and family who I can call on. And I'm learning day by day how to be more open and transparent with them. But this experience taught me about a larger community. There are people out there who you might never have imagined impacting. Community isn't always made up of the people who look like you. I used to talk about my community almost exclusively in terms of Black women. And don't get me wrong, I love us. But the truth is that some of the backlash I received came from women who looked like me. And that was painful, to say the least. I also know, however, that some of that came from a strange kind of protectiveness we often have over each other. We don't want to see another one of us mess up, and when we do, it can be frustrating. I'm thankful, though, that for every Black woman who said, "This bitch was dumb," there were six other Black women who were like, "Hold your head up, queen. We got you." And I'm equally grateful that I learned just how big my community can be. That I can see the world—my world—with new eyes.

So I told myself once I stepped off the plane in California: *If I say nothing else, I will talk about community.* But that was it. What would I say about community? To what extent? Up to the moment before it was my time to speak, I had no idea.

Here's the thing: This wasn't just a speaking engagement. It was the first time I had to stand before people who only knew my story from what they had seen on their phones—people who were sitting just a few feet away from me, watching, waiting, and expecting me to deliver something real. It was the first time I had to honor my truth in real time, with my whole body present. Speaking your truth is not just about words coming out of your mouth; it's also about allowing your whole self to stand unhidden. And for a long time, I had mastered the art of hiding in plain sight.

So in order to prepare myself emotionally, I clung to that one word: *community*.

When asked again about my speech, I told the planners, "My speech will have something to do with community, but . . ." I could see them waiting with anticipation for some kind of detailed breakdown. ". . . I really don't have anything written down." I won't name her, but one of Amplify's directors looked understandably worried. They didn't know what would come out of my mouth—and honestly, neither did I. I was just as freaked out as I think they were. There were no *I can do this* mantras in my head or feelings of empowerment in the moments leading up to my presentation. But there *was* a kind of resolve. I knew I couldn't second-guess myself. I was going to talk from the heart, because that's what has always worked for me.

The next morning, I woke up with a knot in my stomach. Not butterflies but knots. The kind you get when your mind is rehearsing every possible disaster that could happen. *What if I trip onstage? What if I forget what I'm saying? What if they look at me with blank faces? What if my truth is not enough?*

Then there was the suit.

Lord, that blue suit. I had bought it from Macy's thinking it would be perfect because it was bold and powerful. That was the energy I wanted to convey. The only problem was that when I put it on, it didn't fit right. It had fit in the dressing room, but when I put it on the day of the speech, well, the pants were too loose. The waist kept slipping, and I didn't have a belt. My heels were strappy, and suddenly I was hyperaware of every inch of my body. My fat girl worries immediately took center stage: *Please don't let me trip.*

Please don't let my pants fall down. Please don't let my stomach act crazy. Please, Lord, just get me through this. Those dumb, anxious thoughts summed up my entire internal monologue.

It's funny how, in moments of great destiny, your fear will try to distract you with the pettiest of concerns. That's what anxiety does. It zooms in on the smallest detail and makes it bigger than it really is. It makes you focus on the superficial so you don't have to face the soul-level shift taking place.

Backstage, they attached the mic pack to me, and I swore that the producers could hear my heart racing. I could feel it in my throat. The director looked at me with that slightly worried look in her eyes, probably because she still didn't know what I was going to say. I took one last deep breath.

Then I heard it: "Please welcome to the stage Reesa Teesa."

I walked out with my hands in my pockets—not for style, mind you, but because that was literally the only way to hold my pants up. The lights were bright. The room was quiet. All eyes were on me. And I told the truth.

But before I told the truth, I acknowledged it.

"Let me just go ahead and address the elephant in the room," I said. "I am nervous."

As those words left my mouth, something in the atmosphere shifted. I could feel the room breathe with me. In that moment, I realized that honoring my truth didn't start with the dramatic details of my story on TikTok. It started with the honesty of acknowledging where I stood right then: Nervous. Vulnerable. Human. That was the doorway, and I stepped right on through it.

The next words that came out of my mouth weren't rehearsed or polished, and they definitely weren't written on any notecard. I knew there were people who didn't have a clue who I was, so I told them. "My name is Reesa Teesa, and I did a fifty-part TikTok series called 'Who the Fuck Did I Marry?'" There were laughs and claps at that. What came out next was just me, unfiltered and alive. I started talking about community, not as a concept but as the net that caught me when life dropped me. I decided to be honest about what I had faced in the initial days and weeks of the series going viral.

I also shared how my story didn't just resonate with Black women who saw themselves in my pain but with people across the globe who understood betrayal and heartbreak—people who had loved deeply and lost hard.

"I thought my community would only be people who looked like me," I said. And that was true. I know it was my community of sisters, Black women, who had helped the series blow up. I will always be grateful to them and honor that. "But as the series spread, I realized my community was also men in Australia. And mothers in Brazil. Veterans in Toronto. Aunties in Mississippi." I listed certain countries and locations because, according to my TikTok analytics, those were some of the highest-viewing locations, and they came to mind as I spoke. I wanted the audience to understand that community is not necessarily built by superficial similarities like race or ethnicity but can be built by shared truth. My truth, as ugly as it might have been, made room for others to honor theirs. There were people all over the world who knew what it felt like to think it's their turn in love, only to find out it wasn't. To have a relationship blow up in their faces spectacularly.

As I spoke, something clicked. The fear didn't disappear; it transformed. It became energy. And clarity. I finally understood that my TikTok series may have introduced me to the world, but that stage introduced me to myself. And I could feel the audience leaning in, not because I was sensational but because I was sincere. I realized, in that moment, that there is a difference between entertaining an audience and *connecting* with one. On that stage, I was doing the latter.

And I remembered something else too: I had already lived through the worst of it. The humiliation of my failed marriage. The viral explosion of my pain that millions of strangers consumed. But in that room, I wasn't defending myself. I wasn't asking to be believed. I was simply speaking my truth because it was mine to tell. The room didn't feel intimidating anymore. It felt intimate. I wasn't performing; I was *witnessing*. And I was offering up my truth as a mirror so others could see something of themselves in it.

It wasn't a dramatic crescendo. There weren't violins playing in the background or tears streaming down my face. The turning point that occurred for me at Amplify happened as I ended my presentation. "While you're here talking to each other, take a moment to listen. You never know how offering a listening ear can change someone's trajectory, because so many of us just want someone to listen. And that's all I have to say."

The room erupted in applause. I didn't plan that ending. It came out naturally, the way truth often does. Then I saw people rising to their feet: a standing ovation. I was emotionally amped. The voices in my head had changed their tune: *They heard you. They listened. They get it. This is why you're here.* That's when my body nearly gave out—not from fear anymore but from release. It was like God was saying, "Well done. You gave it to Me, and I gave you the words to speak. Always trust Me, Tareasa." I could have cried right then and there.

People often talk about wanting to be seen, but I've learned that what we desire even more deeply is to be *heard*. The series had been born because I was in therapy, but I didn't feel that my therapist was really hearing me. I'd tried the "don't put your business out there" way, but her advice made no sense to me. She wasn't listening, so I stopped going to see her. But I still needed to get everything out. It was *that* frustration that made me pick up the phone and hit RECORD. And walking off that stage at CAA Amplify, I felt like I'd finally been understood. I'd finally been heard.

People can say what they want about me, but I will always be my biggest cheerleader. I flew across the country alone and fought through my self-doubt and my low self-esteem. But I still got my happy high yellow behind on that stage and told a story from the heart without a single note. I didn't stutter. I didn't sound like I was about to cry. My pants didn't fall down. And I didn't trip in those heels. So hell yeah, I walked off that stage proud.

Afterward, several people came up to me and thanked me for my talk—some whose names I recognized and others whose I didn't. But what struck me most wasn't who they were; it was what they said.

"You said what I've been afraid to admit."

"Thank you for naming it."

The next day, at the dinner, people were still coming up to me, shaking my hand, and asking for pictures. Again, I didn't know who most of them were. At one point, a man leaned in and said, "There were only two standing ovations this year."

I said, "Oh."

He said, "You and Michelle Obama."

My heart swelled.

Earlier that day, I had stood and clapped for Michelle Obama after she delivered her presentation. Afterward, I went up to a Secret Service agent and asked, "Is there any way I can meet Mrs. Obama?"

He spoke into his microphone and then asked, "What's your name?"

I almost said Tareasa—especially since that's really who was asking. Then I thought, *Maybe I'll get a little further if I say Reesa Teesa.*

"Reesa Teesa."

It didn't work.

They told me her schedule was too tight and that she was already leaving for her next event. I didn't get to meet Michelle Obama nor Regina King, another favorite of mine. But we were in the same room. And sometimes that is enough.

It was never just about my own courage when I was doing the fifty-part series, when I was standing on that stage, and all the other times I've spoken publicly since. God has been using my story to give other people permission to see their own. For so much of my life, I unconsciously chose to stay small. I didn't always speak up for myself, even when my gut, my spirit, was telling me to. I was willing to settle for a life that was clearly smaller than what God had planned for me. Even when I got glimpses that God wanted more of my presence in the world, I would try to shrink myself. I'd want to retreat just like I did the night before speaking at CAA Amplify. It was important to me to make everyone else feel comfortable—to not ruffle feathers and to keep the peace. But standing on that Amplify stage made me realize that what I had been doing wasn't keeping the peace at all. I don't want to say that the applause and the kudos validated me, but in a way, they did. When you live in a bubble where your world is encompassed in less than one hundred square miles—where you go to work, come home, maybe grab a drink with your friend, and that's it—it's easy to have very narrow views of yourself and of the world. Knowing that my words mattered on a large scale opened my eyes to not just what was possible but what God had put inside me all along. I was done betraying myself.

People often assume that speaking your truth is all about confidence. It's not—at least not entirely. It's mostly about alignment. And it's also about choosing authenticity over approval. It's about deciding that your healing is more important than other people's comfort. I did not walk onto that stage feeling empowered at all. In fact, I walked onto that stage feeling scared as hell. But I *walked off free.* And that's what matters most.

It's not even really about the applause. That was cool, but it wasn't the most important part. The most important part was that I could clap for myself. I could be proud of myself for choosing transparency over performance. My truth was not perfect, but it was *mine.* And I reclaimed a part of me that I think had been waiting years to breathe.

Leaving Amplify, I was starting a new chapter. Now every stage, every interview, and every conversation was an opportunity to practice truth telling.

Even in the process of writing this book, I've said over and over again that I do not have all the answers. Half the time, I struggle with connecting the dots between what happened to me, the choices I made, the healing journey I'm on, and what is happening in my life now. I don't stand before people as a woman who has "arrived," nor do I ever want to. I'm standing as a woman in motion, healing in real time.

I do eventually hope to get to a place where, instead of saying, *Oh my God, what am I doing here?* I can say with confidence, *Honey, you're here because you belong here. You earned your way here.* I still struggle though. When people tell me my series was a cultural phenomenon, it's hard to hold. My reflex is to say, "No, I just told a story of my experience," but I know that's not entirely true. It's been so much bigger. I hope to someday reach a place where I really understand that. I'm not there yet, but at Amplify, I got a peek at what was possible. I understand why I was invited.

I also hope that as I continue, I can get to a place where I'm proud of making "Who TF Did I Marry?" Right now, I still wrestle with the embarrassment of it all. Some of that shame lingers. But I will get there—I can feel it.

If you're reading this right now and wrestling with sharing your own truth because you've either buried it or convinced yourself that silence is safer, I'm here to tell you: There is no freedom in hiding. No, you don't have to tell the whole world your story the way I did. But you *do* owe yourself the gift of honesty. When you choose to honor your truth—as messy, unfinished, or inconvenient as it may be—you will inevitably open the door to healing. I walked off that stage in Ojai, California, not as a woman who had just given a speech but as a woman who had come home to herself. I want that kind of freedom for you too.

13

Through Acceptance, I Am Discovering My Worth

When you are open to learning your worth, everything else falls into place.

I THOUGHT I MIGHT END THIS BOOK by talking about all the ways to embrace our worth. Then I realized that this wouldn't be an authentic point of view—at least not entirely. The truth is, I'm not sure if I know deep down the fullness of my worth. In fact, I'm still discovering it day by day. And I've figured out that God is okay with that. There is no perfection to aspire to. He only requires me to continue seeking Him and to focus on having a relationship with Him. That's what I think this experience allowed me to do: to return to the path God had planned for me all along. There will still be some missteps, I'm sure. As I've been saying, I am a work in progress. But as the saying goes, I can be that and a masterpiece at the same time.

Oh, and that is not a disclaimer. If anything, it is a declaration. An affirmation that this chapter, like my life, is not being written from the mountaintop but from the climb. I am not at the end of the road saying, "Look how far I've come." I am still on the road, still navigating, still stopping to catch my breath, still deciding which direction to go next. If there is anything I can offer you here, it is the truth that healing is not found in perfection; it is found in acceptance.

I accept that I'm still figuring things out. For example, let's consider my recent encounter with Beavis. I know, I know. You might be thinking, *Come on, Reesa! He's still around? The one who broke your heart?* Let me explain.

There's this running joke in my family about Beavis and these damn cookies he used to make for me all the time. He fancies himself a pastry chef, so when we were involved, he used to make these white chocolate chip cookies that could only be described as magically delicious. I'm talking about AH-ddictive. Like, if there was ever a dessert equivalent of a drug, these cookies were it—pure crack. And he was just damn good at baking overall. My mother used to ask him to make pound cakes for her back then too. And he'd do it! Mostly because when he injured his back at work, my mama laid her hands on him and prayed heaven down. Within two months, he was back at work. Ever since then, the joke between me and him has been, "Where's my mama's pound cake for healing your back? And where's my cookies for loving you through it?"

But the truth is, those cookies became something more than dessert for me. They became a symbol. At first, they were a symbol of the sweetness I thought we had, the softness I wanted to believe existed between us, even when it didn't. So when Beavis stopped making them, it was like he stopped feeding that part of me that believed he still cared.

Over the years, whenever Beavis would start talking to me again after he'd broken up with his latest girlfriend, I'd ask, "When are you going to make those cookies again?" He'd laugh and dodge the question or promise to get some to me. After I divorced Legion, the joke was back on. But then at some point, I just stopped asking. After we had our talk in 2022 and he made it clear the reason he could never see a future for us, why was I going to keep asking for something—whether cookies or a relationship—that I was never going to get? Then, in 2024, after the TikTok series blew up and he'd expressed that he thought it was a bad idea for me to put my business "in the street," he finally said to me one day, "I promise you, I'll make your favorite cookies before the year's out."

Of course, December 31 came and went. There were no cookies. In fact, there was very little communication from him besides a text here and there.

I think that's when I knew, deep down, that despite the healing journey I was on, I was still holding on to something. I wasn't holding on to the man, per se. But I was still holding on to the fantasy. Remember, I loved this guy. And sometimes when you've loved someone that long, your heart doesn't just quit. So in early 2025, I did what I'd done with other relationships but never with Beavis. I started praying differently. I said, "God, I know he's not for me. You've made that clear. But there's something still lingering. A desperate hope is still present. Remove him from my life. And please, when You do it, make it not hurt. Take the desire for him away, because only You can."

Fast-forward to October 2025, three weeks prior to me writing these words. I hadn't spoken to Beavis at all since August. I hadn't seen him since 2024. But on a random Sunday, my phone lit up with an unexpected text from him.

BEAVIS: Hey, are you in town this week?

I said yes, even though I probably should've said no. He said he had a "special delivery" for me and wanted to drop it off that Monday. *Okay, fine. Whatever.* I probably should've known better, but there is still a part of me that wants to believe people mean well—that change is possible. Plus, there was a fifty-fifty chance he wasn't going to show up anyway. So when he pulled up to my house on Monday, I just laughed to myself. *Of course he'd actually come this time.*

The first mistake he made was knocking on my door even though there was a huge SUV in my driveway that was clearly not mine. I believe Beavis knew it was possible that I had company, but apparently he didn't care. Second, he tried to open my front door without knocking, just like old times. *Excuse me?*

When I came to the door, I looked at him and said, "I know good and damn well you didn't just try to walk in my house."

He laughed. "I thought you were gonna have it unlocked."

"Nah," I said. "You don't just walk in here. You don't know what you might be stepping into."

Beavis handed me a container, and when I opened it, there were five white chocolate chip cookies inside. *I mean, I guess.* I hadn't seen this man in more than a year. I could tell from the way he was dressed that he hadn't just come to drop something off. He had been planning to stay for a while. *What in the world?*

The problem for him was that I actually *did* have company. Another man (mind your business) was already there. Beavis tried to act surprised when he realized this. I asked him if he saw the car in the driveway, but of course he played it off. "Oh, I thought that was yours."

Chile, please. He knew good and well I wasn't driving a huge SUV like that.

So I called the other guy out from the other room and introduced them. Beavis stuck out his hand and introduced himself very formally. Who introduces themselves by their job title in that kind of setting? But that's typical of him. He always needs to assert his importance.

Now you would think he would have left at this point, but nope, Beavis decided he would hang around. In our conversation, he asked about my mother and my aunt, and he even asked how my little cousin Emma was doing. He brought up old stories and inside jokes. It was like he was dropping little hints just to let the other man know he had a history with me and that he'd been part of my life longer. But every word, every smirk, was all a performance. My guy friend knew it too. He was completely unbothered by Beavis's show, and throughout the conversation he kept scrolling on his phone and chuckling as the show went on.

But me? Well, as I was standing there in my kitchen, arms folded, listening to Beavis make a fool of himself, I heard a whisper in my spirit: *You're done.*

They weren't words of defeat either. They were peaceful—the kind of confirmation that can only come after asking God to take the ache for a person away.

I realized at that moment that I wasn't angry at Beavis. I wasn't even sad. I was just finished. I'd spent years wanting this man. Years convincing myself that if I looked a little different or acted a little different, he'd finally see me the way I saw him. But watching him in that kitchen attempting to play in my face once again, I knew I didn't want it anymore.

When he'd officially overstayed his welcome, I finally said, "Well, look at the time. Thank you so much for the cookies."

He laughed. "You putting me out?"

"Yes," I said. "I am."

And I meant it. He left, and I didn't text or call him. I didn't even eat the cookies either. They sat on my counter for a week until I threw them away. When I told Shawn this, she said, "Those were your favorite. You didn't even taste one?"

"No. Those cookies don't represent love and care anymore. They represent manipulation. I'm not putting that in my body."

And I guess that was my breakthrough. It wasn't some dramatic revelation. As usual, it was quiet. I'm finding that this journey toward acceptance, toward embracing my self-worth, isn't all that loud at all. It's just . . . clear.

Once upon a time, I would've let Beavis come in, sit down, and stay as long as he wanted. I would've convinced myself that maybe this time would be different. But that day, only a few weeks ago, I knew I was worth more than a man who spins the block when things don't work out elsewhere. I'm more than the woman who gets chosen by default.

The best way I can describe it is this: Beavis was and is never going to choose me. Nothing I did or can do would ever make him see me the way I saw him. Nothing I did would make him choose me over whoever else comes into his life at a particular time. I've accepted that. And that is half the battle for me. I move differently now. I recognize now that just because I've changed does not mean he has. I know those cookies represented the game he thought we were still playing. The one where maybe he gets sex (though that ended a long time ago), or emotional support, which he still wants.

I knew immediately the cookies were never about cookies. They were a doorway. They were his way of saying, "Come on, TJ. I'm available. It's safe now. Pour into me. Eat this. Be impressed by the effort. Let's pick up where we left off in 2022 or 2023. Give me more of your time and attention. Your emotional labor. So I can fuel myself enough to go back out into the world and find someone new."

Hell no.

I've said it before, and I'll say it again: As much as I struggle with self-worth, the one thing I know is that I don't want to be anybody's experiment anymore. I don't want to be loved just because every other option fell through. I deserve more than to be somebody's yo-yo, the favorite toy they put away and pick back up when they're bored or broken, which was always Beavis's MO. I want to be chosen freely and without hesitation.

Recently, there was a time when, if Beavis called, I would probably have still answered. If someone in his family had passed, I would have still shown up and gone to the funeral. It's been a journey to heal that part of me that still wants to be connected. But I'm grateful for this most recent experience, because at least now I can see the difference between compassion and attachment. I can see how far I've come.

I have finally made a decision regarding Beavis. In order for me to fully "accept" the lesson that has been staring me in the face for years now, I will have to do something very difficult. I will have to remove all access that exists between us. So I have made the choice to block him. I am closing that chapter in my life. I know now I can wish him well and pray for God's protection over him without us being in each other's lives. That's taken a lot for me to do, especially since I considered him a friend. But this recent experience showed me that I will be the default for him, and I can't do that to myself anymore. I can no longer hope and wish for a different outcome. Instead, I will walk away *and* close the door behind me as I leave.

Acceptance can mean so many things, but in this instance, it has meant not needing to announce my goodbye, no matter how long it takes to unfold. It's throwing away the cookies I once begged for. And it's recognizing that my worth doesn't shrink just because someone else couldn't see it.

My self-worth took the biggest hits throughout all my romantic relationships, but the biggest one was in my marriage. In my reflections, though, I realize it was never a one-way street. If we're going to pull back all the layers, the truth is that if I had known my worth for real, the first time that man lied to me would have been the last. I would have been unafraid to say, "This is not for me. So I wish you all the best, but you are not the guy." If I really knew my self-worth, the first time Dallas called me a bitch would have been the last conversation we ever had. If I really knew my self-worth, I would not have let the peer pressure of *You're thirty-five, it's getting late. If you want to have a baby, hurry up* cause me to engage in something that was never for me. I would've known, *I am worth the wait. I am worth making sure I meet the right guy and not being so quick to get married just so I can have a baby to fit what society says is the right time.*

While all this may be true, that doesn't mean I have to live in the shame of it. It was once a fact, but it doesn't have to continue to be. I know now that time is a teacher, yes, but it is also a healer. Every day, every week, my self-worth gets bigger and stronger. I do believe I'm worthy of a pure, healthy, and honest love. Not a struggle love. Not a love that shape-shifts into something awful and unrecognizable. I deserve a healthy, happy relationship. I am absolutely worth a man saying, "I'm going to do right by her because she's worth it."

But in the meantime, I must sit with myself and figure out what to do with the desires of my heart. There have been so many moments when I've had to face parts of my life I never imagined I'd be living—not because I didn't dream big enough but because I dreamed too *specifically*. I had a very clear picture of how I thought things would go: Marriage. Children. A partner to travel with. Family dinners. Matching Christmas pajamas. I held those dreams in my heart for so long that they felt more like destiny than a dream. And when that picture shattered, I didn't just grieve the end of a singular relationship, I had to grieve the end of the *life I thought I was promised*. But accepting that my life has not gone according to plan is not the same as saying my life is over. It is simply acknowledging what is real in this moment: The trajectory has shifted. My timeline is totally different than what I imagined. And that's okay.

I've learned that there are levels to acceptance. For instance, there are things I can accept easily: That I am more recognizable now when I go out in public. That people connect with me because my story helped them tell their own. That who I am, where I live, and how I work are completely different from two years ago. Those things I can accept with relative peace.

But then there's the harder layer. This is where Little Reesa still lives. The girl who, since childhood, believed wholeheartedly that she would grow up, fall in love, get married, and have a baby. The girl who believed that this was simply what *happened* when you were a good person, when you did things "the right way." Letting go of *that* picture is the part that feels like trying to pry my fingers away from something I've held on to my entire life.

I turned forty on February 15, 2025. I woke up at a beautiful resort in the Dominican Republic alone. Yes, I had prepared myself mentally for this—hence the trip—but when the moment hit, it hit hard. I sat there and allowed myself to cry. The tears flowed freely and marked the time very clearly for me. You see, acceptance of your reality, one you didn't choose, sometimes starts with grief. In that space, I said to myself, *You are forty. You may have to accept that the train has left the station.* The train being both marriage and motherhood.

It wasn't that I believed love was now impossible for me. I didn't then, and I don't now. It was just that I realized I have to accept that love may not come in the form or timeline I grew up imagining. Motherhood was and is tied to many complexities I cannot ignore, especially because I know, with full self-awareness, that I still do not want to be a single parent. Yes, I know there is a difference between co-parenting and being a single parent. But I don't want that for myself. When I grieved the dream on my birthday, and when I talk about acceptance now, I am not just saying, *Maybe I won't have children.* I am saying, *Maybe I won't have the version of motherhood I always imagined. Maybe true acceptance looks like refusing to pass down my own childhood pain.* So as far as having biological children, at this point, acceptance is telling me that may not be my story. It's not because God can't do it but because my peace cannot be dependent on whether or not He does.

Full disclosure, I do sometimes wonder if I'm even on the list for a happily ever after. That may sound really depressing, but I also feel like it's real. Maybe you've wondered the same about yourself? We know we have good hearts. We know we are good people. But we haven't met the right person, and as life goes on, we aren't sure we ever will. *Am I on the happily ever after list?* It's a quiet question, one I rarely say out loud because it feels too vulnerable, too raw. But this is the final chapter of this book, so I am saying it now.

When my story went public, I worried that I had put a dark cloud over myself. *What man in his right mind*, I thought, *is going to want to deal with a woman who comes with this kind of baggage?* But then an answer rose up to meet that fear: *A healthy man, the right man, will see me as whole, not broken. He will see me as wise, not wounded. He will recognize that what I carry is not baggage but simply evidence of my survival.* This was a refreshing feeling instead of living in the fear and letting it guide me.

I am not closing the door on love. But I am accepting that I am no longer desperate for it. I don't have the luxury of thinking the way I used to think before 2020, when I met Legion. The girl that I was before him is gone. I see all my relationships, romantic or otherwise, differently. And I refuse to run to online dating. I refuse to put myself in places God would not have placed me naturally. So if love comes, it will arrive on God's timing, not on the algorithm's.

Every day, I wake up in a life I never thought I would be living. I never thought I'd be traveling solo, buying real estate solo, going to weddings and baby showers as a single guest rather than hosting my own. And I won't lie: some days I still break down. I still avoid baby showers. I still feel the sting when a friend says, "Will you be my bridesmaid?" Because even in my joy for them, I must accept the ache that whispers, *I wish it were my turn.* Acceptance doesn't eliminate the ache I feel sometimes. It simply allows it to exist without letting it consume me.

This isn't resignation. I think of it as reconstruction. Acceptance doesn't mean giving up on joy, at least to me. I'm just releasing the version of joy I was taught to worship. I'm not so much saying, *That will never happen for me.* I'm saying, *I will no longer wait to live until it happens.*

Right now, acceptance for you, friend, might look like acknowledging that you are still becoming. What are you becoming, exactly? Who knows? I guess that's the point. I know I'm allowing myself to be shaped by God in a way that only a Creator can. And I'm teaching myself to accept that. Tomorrow acceptance might look like something softer, or stronger, or entirely new. Just remember that acceptance itself has layers. It is an onion, and some days peeling it will make you cry. Other days peeling it might feel like freedom. So in this instance, maybe worth is something we *live into* as we accept where we are at any given moment.

So where does that leave me? Definitely not at the end. It feels more like being at a beginning I never expected. I am not closing this book by promising a miracle ending. There is no nice, neat bow to wrap this all up in. That would be dishonest. If there is one thing this journey has taught me, it is that truth, even when it is unfinished, is still sacred. And you know what really gives me joy? The fact that I'm not yet the woman I'm going to be when I come to the other side of this healing journey. That is a glorious expectation. The best is yet to come.

What I do know is that, through acceptance, I am *discovering* my worth. I know what I won't tolerate again, and for me, that's a wonderful starting point. And no, I might not have yet reached that elusive destination called "healed," but I am finally willing to stand still long enough to see what has been true all along.

What TF do I do now? I keep rebuilding. I keep picking up the pieces of my life and throwing away the ones that no longer fit. The people pleasing, the desperation, the timelines, and the external validation—those go in the discard pile. The pieces that get to stay are my voice, my strength, my discernment, my peace, my laughter, my solitude, my community, and my healing. And maybe, just maybe, the fullness of my worth will be revealed in the process.

A Love Letter to the Old Me

DEAR 2026 REESA,

Girl, I am so proud of us! I won't lie—for a minute, you had me worried we weren't going to make it. I was concerned that we would never get to the place I am currently in, because you weren't moving fast enough toward the mental, emotional, and spiritual place where you needed to be. Boy, was I wrong! Looking back, I am amazed at how we turned our lemons into lemonade. We have always been strong, that's for sure, but we had never really been battle-tested. Now we have been. We have always had a voice, but unfortunately, we only used it around our inner circle, the family and friends who were closest to us, and sometimes not even then. Now it's being heard worldwide! Who would've thought the little girl from Willingboro, New Jersey, the young teen from Marietta, Georgia, the young woman at Florida A&M University, or the grown woman who worked at Georgia State Patrol would create something so courageous, so monumental, so groundbreaking, that our name is being spoken in rooms we never dreamt of?

Well, God did.

I'm so proud you made a decision that we both know our younger self would NEVER have made. You chose to embrace the rubble that your life became, share your story, own it, and, most importantly, learn from it. I wouldn't be here with this glorious life if you hadn't done those things. We were made to be more than someone's spouse living a life she didn't want nor deserve. You decided to say, "I deserve better," and while it took some time, you didn't just stay and accept the lies. For that, I salute you.

You asked "What TF do I do now?" Well, honey, you rebuilt your life, piece by piece, and now we are thriving. This book did amazing numbers. You will be pleased to know you are a best-selling author. And we've gone on to publish more. Our stories have been helping people worldwide. We will speak in front of thousands of people, and our confidence has only grown. Grandma would be so proud of us. Remember how she taught us to enunciate our words back in the day? Hell, we speak so well because she taught us.

I almost forgot to tell you about the TV show! Girl, the process paid off. I know you were worried in the beginning, but it all worked out. That thing did so well that multiple seasons were birthed from it—and you are an executive producer on every episode. Our name is in the credits because of what you did. Periodt! You will be nominated for Emmys, spoken-word Grammys, and so many other prestigious awards. But the best part is that we've done all this while remaining the same funny, up-to-her-crazy-antics Tareasa.

No, this journey has not been easy. Many days, you weren't sure it would work out. But from this side of our life, I can confidently say to you, "It was all worth it." You dared to not stay quiet, and you chose not to live in shame. You recognized that what you went through was simply a chapter in our book of life and that it deserved to be told. Now it's true that not all the decisions you made were good, nor were they wise. We both know that. But they were ours to make. And they shaped you into the woman we are at this moment. The dream we dreamt at ten years old didn't quite pan out the way we thought, right? But look at us now: living a life our eyes hadn't seen, our ears had never heard.

I love you. Always have. But more importantly, I can't say enough how proud of you I am. I've never looked back at you and felt ashamed or embarrassed because I know I wouldn't be here if you hadn't been you—on purpose.

LOVE,
FUTURE REESA

Acknowledgments

This book was such a raw and personal journey. It is not easy to open up for the world to see the real sides of you. The beautiful and ugly parts. The pain. And in order to sit down and get this book from a thought to a bookstore shelf, it takes a lot of hard work. It cannot be done alone, yet I'm clear that the critiques and praise will be felt by me alone as the author. There are people who poured into me, and, let's be real, there are some who took parts of me. Yet, all of that is what has made me.

To my family and friends: I group you all together because, collectively, you all are my "village." Thank you for loving me when I barely loved myself. Thank you for guiding me when I was blind and couldn't see the road, let alone the destination. Thank you for pushing me when I sat down because I was too tired to push myself. Thank you for covering me even when I felt naked, alone, and scared. This book would not have happened if it wasn't for my village of family and true friends who stood with me when the world tried to make me a hashtag.

To Omara: I thank you for being the attorney every client deserves. You were the person who returned my phone call in February 2024 when no other attorney would call this unknown woman back. You are the one who has faithfully negotiated, advocated, and fought for my interests since day one. You have never treated me as less than because my contracts might have been small. You celebrate my big wins and my small victories. You have always been an ear to vent to and a vault for my confidential fears. And while I do still want that LV purse you have, I am more grateful to you because you still have my back. Thank you.

To Jenn Baker and the entire Storehouse Voices team: Having a publishing team who looks like you, sounds like you, and hears you is a blessing. Thank you, Jenn, for all your notes and emails. I know that you were doing all you can to push this book to its fullest potential. Thank you to Storehouse for even being willing to take this on. For wanting to be a part of bringing my baby to the world. Finally, thank you all for honoring the integrity of this story and for never trying to make it into something it isn't.

To Michael, Kristyn, and the team at CAA: People will never know just how hard we fought to even make this book. Every Zoom meeting and phone call, every email exchange, the two of you were right by my side. You carefully explained the process and stood ten toes deep with me when it came to writing this book. Both of you have been some of my biggest advocates, and I deeply thank you for always being just an email away when I needed clarity or to share my thoughts. Signing with CAA was one of the best decisions I made, and you are a testament to that. Thank you to everyone at CAA who had a hand in making this book possible.

To the EPs (Harlin, Wilson, Snowden, and Roberts): You all drove me crazy (LOL). Pure and simple, you drove me up the wall! There were times I didn't know who worked with who or for whom, but one thing is for sure, you all took care of me when I needed it most. From Los Angeles to New York (and even a stop in Texas), you four traveled with me and made sure I was okay. Thank you for treating me as "Tareasa" and, when I got to be too much, for bringing me back to reality. Thank you for encouraging me when I get nervous for a film shoot and making sure my clothes fit for a photo shoot. Thank you for whisking me away in a heat wave so I didn't pass out and for traveling last minute across the ocean and staying by my side. No matter what was going on, I knew I was okay because you all were there. You don't hear it enough and I can't say it enough: Thank you!

To the CCSO: It's a little bittersweet writing this. This job opened the door for me to discover the truth that led me down the road I am currently on. When my life felt like it was falling apart, I had a boss who said, "We got your back." And that meant so much to me. However, I would be remiss if I did not thank the people who allowed me to go "here, there, and everywhere" and keep my job. The people who truly let me be "Reesa Teesa" and "Tareasa Johnson" at the same time. The days when my two worlds collided, they gave me the grace to handle both. A lot of jobs would not have worked with me the way the CCSO did. I am forever grateful to all the people who helped build me up and let me be me. Too many names to list, but just know, I thank you all.

To Tracey M. Lewis-Giggetts: As the collaborator on this book, you and I have a unique relationship. I'm going to write this a little differently, so follow me:

Thank you for your ears. You actually listened to me, not just heard me.

Thank you for your eyes. You saw me as a person; a real woman who was trying to get her story out and not some social media caricature. You didn't see me as damaged goods, but as a woman being made whole.

Thank you for your hands. You wrote words that my mind couldn't think of. You took time to carefully express things I was struggling to say.

Thank you for your mouth. You spoke life into me. You may not have even known but there were times when I know beyond a shadow of a doubt you were sent to speak into me. There were times I was too EXHAUSTED to even get on a Zoom meeting with you and by the time it was done, I felt like I could conquer anything.

I thank you and I honor the gift you have. You were the perfect fit and the right person, at the right time, to collaborate with on this book. If this book is my baby, you, ma'am, were my doula. And yes, I know you wanted to slap me upside the head (a few times), but I'm okay with that. I am truly all the better because I have had the privilege and honor to work with you.

LASTLY, AND I MEAN THIS with all my heart, to the people who watched "Who TF Did I Marry?" and found themselves relating to my story; to the people who sent me DMs, emails, texts, phone calls, and everything in between, just to say some words of encouragement; to the women and men who in the quietness of your heart felt like you were "the only one" but now see that you were not alone: I say, THANK YOU. This book would not have been written if it had not been for you all.

About the Author

TAREASA M. JOHNSON, professionally known as Reesa Teesa, is an American content creator and storyteller recognized for her compelling digital narratives and global cultural impact. Born in Willingboro, New Jersey, and raised in Marietta, Georgia, she brings a unique perspective that is shaped by both her East Coast roots and Southern upbringing. She is a graduate of Kennesaw State University, where she earned a degree in Criminal Justice and completed a study abroad program in The Hague, where she focused on International Law and Counterterrorism. She spent several years working in law enforcement administration prior to transitioning to content creation.

Johnson rose to international prominence in 2024 with her viral TikTok narrative, "Who TF Did I Marry?"—a fifty-part storytelling series that chronicled a personal relationship marked by significant deception. Her clear, engaging delivery and candid reflections resonated with a global audience, generating more than 450 million views and impressions and prompting widespread conversations about personal accountability, emotional resilience, and self-worth.

In addition to her success as a digital creator, Johnson is a passionate writer who values storytelling as both a professional craft and personal outlet. She also enjoys exploring culinary experiences and sharing thoughtful restaurant reviews in her free time, reflecting her appreciation for culture and community. An avid traveler, Johnson has visited destinations including London, Paris, and South Africa—experiences that continue to influence her perspective and creative voice.

Following her rapid rise, she has appeared on major national and international platforms such as *Good Morning America* and *Tamron Hall.* She is represented by Creative Artists Agency (CAA) and is currently developing a scripted television adaptation of her story, with Natasha Rothwell attached to star and produce.

Through her work, Johnson continues to demonstrate the power of authentic storytelling, using her platform to engage and inspire audiences while redefining how personal narratives can shape broader cultural conversations.

About Storehouse Voices

STOREHOUSE VOICES celebrates culturally rich narratives that reflect the dynamic influence of communities across the globe. Our imprint is dedicated to amplifying underrepresented and over-worthy voices in fiction and nonfiction, with a focus on accessible and engaging content that honors the past, disrupts the present, and imagines new futures.